A Little Book
of Western Verse

Eugene Field

Contents

A LITTLE BOOK
OF WESTERN VERSE

BY

Eugene Field

TO MARY FIELD FRENCH.

A dying mother gave to you
Her child a many years ago;
How in your gracious love he grew,
You know, dear, patient heart, you know.

The mother's child you fostered then
Salutes you now and bids you take
These little children of his pen
And love them for the author's sake.

To you I dedicate this book,
And, as you read it line by line,
Upon its faults as kindly look
As you have always looked on mine.

Tardy the offering is and weak;—
Yet were I happy if I knew
These children had the power to speak
My love and gratitude to you.
E. F.

Go, little book; and if an one would speak thee ill, let him bethink him that thou art the child of one who loves thee well.

A Little Book of Western Verse

CASEY'S TABLE D'HÔTE.

OH, them days on Red Hoss Mountain, when the skies wuz fair 'nd blue,
When the money flowed like likker, 'nd the folks wuz brave 'nd true!
When the nights wuz crisp 'nd balmy, 'nd the camp wuz all astir,
With the joints all throwed wide open 'nd no sheriff to demur!
Oh, them times on Red Hoss Mountain in the Rockies fur away,—
There's no sich place nor times like them as I kin find to-day!
What though the camp hes busted? I seem to see it still
A-lyin', like it loved it, on that big 'nd warty hill;
And I feel a sort of yearnin' 'nd a chokin' in my throat
When I think of Red Hoss Mountain 'nd of Casey's tabble dote!

Wal, yes; it's true I struck it rich, but that don't cut a show
When one is old 'nd feeble 'nd it's nigh his time to go;
The money that he's got in bonds or carries to Invest
Don't figger with a codger who has lived a life out West;
Us old chaps like to set around, away from folks 'nd noise,
'Nd think about the sights we seen and things we done when boys;
The which is why I love to set 'nd think of them old days
When all us Western fellers got the Colorado craze,—
And that is why I love to set around all day 'nd gloat
On thoughts of Red Hoss Mountain 'nd of Casey's tabble dote.
This Casey wuz an Irishman,—you 'd know it by his name
And by the facial features appertainin' to the same.
He 'd lived in many places 'nd had done a thousand things,
From the noble art of actin' to the work of dealin' kings,
But, somehow, had n't caught on; so, driftin' with the rest,
He drifted for a fortune to the undeveloped West,
And he come to Red Hoss Mountain when the little camp wuz new,
When the money flowed like likker, 'nd the folks wuz brave 'nd true;

And, havin' been a Stewart on a Mississippi boat,
He opened up a caffy 'nd he run a tabble dote.

The bar wuz long 'nd rangey, with a mirrer on the shelf,
'Nd a pistol, so that Casey, when required, could help himself;
Down underneath there wuz a row of bottled beer 'nd wine,
'Nd a kag of Burbun whiskey of the run of '59;

Upon the walls wuz pictures of hosses 'nd of girls,—
Not much on dress, perhaps, but strong on records 'nd on curls!
The which had been identified with Casey in the past,—
The hosses 'nd the girls, I mean,—and both wuz mighty fast!
But all these fine attractions wuz of precious little note
By the side of what wuz offered at Casey's tabble dote.
There wuz half-a-dozen tables altogether in the place,
And the tax you had to pay upon your vittles wuz a case;
The boardin'-houses in the camp protested 't wuz a shame
To patronize a robber, which this Casey wuz the same!
They said a case was robbery to tax for ary meal;
But Casey tended strictly to his biz, 'nd let 'em squeal;
And presently the boardin'-houses all began to bust,
While Casey kept on sawin' wood 'nd layin' in the dust;
And oncet a trav'lin' editor from Denver City wrote
A piece back to his paper, puffin' Casey's tabble dote.

A tabble dote is different from orderin' aller cart:
In one case you git all there is, in t' other, only part!
And Casey's tabble dote began in French,—as all begin,—
And Casey's ended with the same, which is to say, with "vin;"
But in between wuz every kind of reptile, bird, 'nd beast,
The same like you can git in high-toned restauraws down east;
'Nd windin' up wuz cake or pie, with coffee demy tass,
Or, sometimes, floatin' Ireland in a soothin' kind of Sass

That left a sort of pleasant ticklin' in a feller's throat,
'Nd made him hanker after more of Casey's tabble dote.
The very recollection of them puddin's 'nd them pies
Brings a yearnin' to my buzzum 'nd the water to my eyes;
'Nd seems like cookin' nowadays aint what it used to be
In camp on Red Hoss Mountain in that year of '63;
But, maybe, it is better, 'nd, maybe, I 'm to blame—
I 'd like to be a-livin' in the mountains jest the same—
I 'd like to live that life again when skies wuz fair 'nd blue,
When things wuz run wide open 'nd men wuz brave 'nd true;
When brawny arms the flinty ribs of Red Hoss Mountain smote
For wherewithal to pay the price of Casey's tabble dote.

And you, O cherished brother, a-sleepin' way out west,
With Red Hoss Mountain huggin' you close to its lovin' breast,—
Oh, do you dream in your last sleep of how we use to do,
Of how we worked our little claims together, me 'nd you?
Why, when I saw you last a smile wuz restin' on your face,
Like you wuz glad to sleep forever in that lonely place;
And so you wuz, 'nd I 'd be, too, if I wuz sleepin' so.
But, bein' how a brother's love aint for the world to know,
Whenever I 've this heartache 'nd this chokin' in my throat,
I lay it all to thinkin' of Casey's tabble dote.

LITTLE BOY BLUE.

THE little toy dog is covered with dust,
But sturdy and stanch he stands;
And the little toy soldier is red with rust,
And his musket moulds in his hands.
Time was when the little toy dog was new
And the soldier was passing fair,
And that was the time when our Little Boy Blue

Kissed them and put them there.

"Now, don't you go till I come," he said,
"And don't you make any noise!"
So toddling off to his trundle-bed
He dreamt of the pretty toys.
And as he was dreaming, an angel song
Awakened our Little Boy Blue,—
Oh, the years are many, the years are long,
But the little toy friends are true.

Ay, faithful to Little Boy Blue they stand,
Each in the same old place,
Awaiting the touch of a little hand,
The smile of a little face.
And they wonder, as waiting these long years through,
In the dust of that little chair,
What has become of our Little Boy Blue
Since he kissed them and put them there.

MADGE: YE HOYDEN.

I.

AT Madge, ye hoyden, gossips scofft,
Ffor that a romping wench was shee—
"Now marke this rede," they bade her oft,
"Forsooken sholde your folly bee!"
But Madge, ye hoyden, laught & cried,
"Oho, oho," in girlish glee,
And noe thing mo replied.

II.

No griffe she had nor knew no care,
But gayly rompit all daies long,
And, like ye brooke that everywhere
Goes jinking with a gladsome song,
Shee danct and songe from morn till night,—
Her gentil harte did know no wrong,
Nor did she none despight.

III.

Sir Tomas from his noblesse halle
Did trend his path a somer's daye;
And to ye hoyden he did call
And these ffull evill words did say:
"O wolde you weare a silken gown
And binde your haire with ribands gay?
Then come with me to town!"

IV.

But Madge, ye hoyden, shoke her head,—
" I 'le be no lemman unto thee
For all your golde and gownes," shee said,
"Ffor Robin hath bespoken mee."
Then ben Sir Tomas sore despight,
And back unto his hall went hee
With face as ashen white.

V.

"O Robin, wilt thou wed this girl,
Whenas she is so vaine a sprite?
"So spak ffull many an envious churle
Unto that curteyse countrie wight.
But Robin did not pay no heede;
And they ben wed a somer night & danct upon ye meade.

VI.
Then scarse ben past a yeare & daye
Whan Robin toke unto his bed,
And long, long time therein he lay,
Nor colde not work to earn his bread;
in soche an houre, whan times ben sore,
Sr. Tomas came with haughtie tread & knockit at ye doore.

VII.

Saies: "Madge, ye hoyden, do you know
how that you once despighted me?
But He forgiff an you will go
my swete harte lady ffor to bee!"
But Madge, ye hoyden, heard noe more,—
straightway upon her heele turnt shee,
& shote ye cottage doore.

VIII.

Soe Madge, ye hoyden, did her parte
whiles that ye years did come and go;
't was somer allwais in her harte,

tho' winter strewed her head with snowe.
She toilt and span thro' all those years
nor bid repine that it ben soe,
nor never shad noe teares.

IX.

Whiles Robin lay within his bed,
A divell came and whispered lowe,—
"Giff you will doe my will," he said,
"None more of sickness you shall knowe!"
Ye which gave joy to Robin's soul—
Saies Robin: " Divell, be it soe,
an that you make me whoale!"

X.

That day, upp rising ffrom his bed,
Quoth Robin: "I am well again!"
& backe he came as from ye dead,
& he ben mickle blithe as when
he wooed his doxy long ago;
& Madge did make ado & then
Her teares ffor joy did flowe.
XI.

Then came that hell-born cloven thing—
Saies: "Robin, I do claim your life,
and I hencefoorth shall be your king,
and you shall do my evill strife.
Look round about and you shall see
sr. Tomas' young and ffoolish wiffe—
a comely dame is shee!"

XII.

Ye divell had him in his power,
and not colde Robin say thereto:
Soe Robin from that very houre
did what that divell bade him do;
He wooed and clipt, and on a daye
sr. Tomas' wife and Robin flewe
a many leagues away.

XIII.

Sir Tomas ben wood wroth and swore,
And sometime strode thro' leaf & brake
and knockit at ye cottage door
and thus to Madge, ye hoyden, spake:
Saies, " I wolde have you ffor mine own,
So come with mee & bee my make,
syn tother birds ben flown."

XIV.

But Madge, ye hoyden, bade him noe;
Saies: "Robin is my swete harte still,
And, tho' he doth despight me soe,
I mean to do him good for ill.
So goe, Sir Tomas, goe your way;
ffor whiles I bee on live I will
ffor Robin's coming pray!"

XV.

Soe Madge, ye hoyden, kneelt & prayed
that Godde sholde send her Robin backe.
And tho' ye folke vast scoffing made,
and tho' ye worlde ben colde and blacke,
And tho', as moneths dragged away,
ye hoyden's harte ben like to crack
With griff, she still did praye.

XVI.

Sicke of that divell's damnèd charmes,
Aback did Robin come at last,
And Madge, ye hoyden, sprad her arms
and gave a cry and held him fast;
And as she clong to him and cried,
her patient harte with joy did brast,
& Madge, ye hoyden, died.

OLD ENGLISH LULLABY.

HUSH, bonnie, dinna greit;
Moder will rocke her sweete,—
Balow, my boy!
When that his toile ben done,
Daddie will come anone,—
Hush thee, my lyttel one;
Balow, my boy!

Gin thou dost sleepe, perchaunce
Fayries will come to daunce,—

Balow, my boy!
Oft hath thy moder seene
Moonlight and mirkland queene
Daunce on thy slumbering een,—
Balow, my boy!

Then droned a bumblebee
Saftly this songe to thee:
"Balow, my boy!"

And a wee heather bell,
Pluckt from a fayry dell,
Chimed thee this rune hersell:
"Balow, my boy!"

Soe, bonnie, dinna greit;
Moder doth rock her sweete,—
Balow, my boy!
Give mee thy lyttel hand,
Moder will hold it and
Lead thee to balow land,—
Balow, my boy!

THE BIBLIOMANIAC'S PRAYER.

KEEP me, I pray, in wisdom's way
That I may truths eternal seek;
I need protecting care to-day,—
My purse is light, my flesh is weak.
So banish from my erring heart
All baleful appetites and hints
Of Satan's fascinating art,
Of first editions, and of prints.

Direct me in some godly walk
Which leads away from bookish strife,
That I with pious deed and talk
May extra-illustrate my life.

But if, O Lord, it pleaseth Thee
To keep me in temptation's way,
I humbly ask that I may be
Most notably beset to-day;
Let my temptation be a book,
Which I shall purchase, hold, and keep,

Whereon when other men shall look,
They 'll wail to know I got it cheap.
Oh, let it such a volume be
As in rare copperplates abounds,
Large paper, clean, and fair to see,
Uncut, unique, unknown to Lowndes.

THE LYTTEL BOY.

SOMETIME there ben a lyttel boy
That wolde not renne and play,
And helpless like that little tyke
Ben allwais in the way.
"Goe, make you merrie with the rest,"
His weary moder cried;
But with a frown he catcht her gown
And hong untill her side.
That boy did love his moder well,
Which spake him faire, I ween;
He loved to stand and hold her hand
And ken her with his een;

His cosset bleated in the croft,
His toys unheeded lay,—
He wolde not goe, but, tarrying soe,
Ben allwais in the way.

Godde loveth children and doth gird
His throne with soche as these,
And He doth smile in plaisaunce while
They cluster at His knees;
And sometime, when He looked on earth
And watched the bairns at play,
He kenned with joy a lyttel boy
Ben allwais in the way.

And then a moder felt her heart
How that it ben to-torne,—
She kissed eche day till she ben gray
The shoon he use to worn;
No bairn let hold untill her gown
Nor played upon the floore,—
Godde's was the joy; a lyttel boy
Ben in the way no more!

THE TRUTH ABOUT HORACE.

IT is very aggravating
To hear the solemn prating
Of the fossils who are stating
That old Horace was a prude;
When we know that with the ladies
He was always raising Hades,
And with many an escapade his
Best productions are imbued.

There's really not much harm in a
Large number of his carmina,
But these people find alarm in a
Few records of his acts;
So they 'd squelch the muse caloric,
And to students sophomoric
They 'd present as metaphoric
What old Horace meant for facts.

We have always thought 'em lazy;
Now we adjudge 'em crazy!
Why, Horace was a daisy
That was very much alive!
And the wisest of us know him
As his Lydia verses show him,—
Go, read that virile poem,—
It is No. 25.

He was a very owl, sir,
And starting out to prowl, sir,
You bet he made Rome howl, sir,
Until he filled his date;
With a massic-laden ditty
And a classic maiden pretty
He painted up the city,
And Maecenas paid the freight!

THE DEATH OF ROBIN HOOD.

"GIVE me my bow," said Robin Hood,
"An arrow give to me;
And where 't is shot mark thou that spot,

For there my grave shall be."

Then Little John did make no sign,
And not a word he spake;
But he smiled, altho' with mickle woe
His heart was like to break.

He raised his master in his arms,
And set him on his knee;
And Robin's eyes beheld the skies,
The shaws, the greenwood tree.

The brook was babbling as of old,
The birds sang full and clear,
And the wild-flowers gay like a carpet lay
In the path of the timid deer.

"O Little John," said Robin Hood,
"Meseemeth now to be
Standing with you so stanch and true
Under the greenwood tree.

"And all around I hear the sound
Of Sherwood long ago,
And my merry men come back again,—
You know, sweet friend, you know!

"Now mark this arrow; where it falls,
When I am dead dig deep,
And bury me there in the greenwood where
I would forever sleep."

He twanged his bow. Upon its course

The clothyard arrow sped,
And when it fell in yonder dèll,
Brave Robin Hood was dead.

The sheriff sleeps in a marble vault,
The king in a shroud of gold;
And upon the air with a chanted pray'r
Mingles the mock of mould.

But the deer draw to the shady pool,
The birds sing blithe and free,
And the wild-flow'rs bloom o'er a hidden tomb
Under the greenwood tree.

"LOLLYBY, LOLLY, LOLLYBY."

LAST night, whiles that the curfew bell ben ringing,
I heard a moder to her dearie singing
"Lollyby, lolly, lollyby."
And presently that chylde did cease hys weeping,
And on his moder's breast did fall a-sleeping,
To "lolly, lolly, lollyby."

Faire ben the chylde unto his moder clinging,
But fairer yet the moder's gentle singing,—
"Lollyby, lolly, lollyby."
And angels came and kisst the dearie smiling
In dreems while him hys moder ben beguiling
With "lolly, lolly, lollyby!"

Then to my harte sales I, " Oh, that thy beating
Colde be assuaged by some swete voice repeating
'Lollyby, lolly, lollyby;'

That like this lyttel chylde I, too, ben sleeping
With plaisaunt phantasies about me creeping,
To lolly, lolly, lollyby!' "

Sometime—mayhap when curfew bells are ringing—
A weary harte shall heare straunge voices singing,
"Lollyby, lolly, lollyby;"
Sometime, mayhap, with Chrysts love round me streaming,
I shall be lulled into eternal dreeming
With "lolly, lolly, lollyby."

HORACE AND LYDIA RECONCILED.

HORACE.

WHEN you were mine in auld lang syne,
And when none else your charms might ogle,
I'll not deny,
Fair nymph, that I
Was happier than a Persian mogul.

LYDIA.

Before she came—that rival flame!—
(Was ever female creature sillier?)
In those good times,
Bepraised in rhymes,
I was more famed than Mother Ilia!

HORACE.

Chloe of Thrace! With what a grace

Does she at song or harp employ her!
I 'd gladly die
If only I
Might live forever to enjoy her!

LYDIA.

My Sybaris so noble is
That, by the gods! I love him madly—
That I might save
Him from the grave
I 'd give my life, and give it gladly!

HORACE.

What if ma belle from favor fell,
And I made up my mind to shake her,
Would Lydia, then,
Come back again
And to her quondam flame betake her?

LYDIA.

My other beau should surely go,
And you alone should find me gracious;
For no one slings
Such odes and things
As does the lauriger Horatius!

OUR TWO OPINIONS.

US two wuz boys when we fell out,—
Nigh to the age uv my youngest now;

Don't rec'lect what 'twuz about,
Some small deeff'rence, I'll allow.
Lived next neighbors twenty years,
A-hatin' each other, me 'nd Jim,—
He havin' his opinyin uv me,
'Nd I havin' my opinyin uv him.

Grew up together 'nd would n't speak,
Courted sisters, 'nd marr'd 'em, too;
'Tended same meetin'-house oncet a week,
A-hatin' each other through 'nd through!
But when Abe Linkern asked the West
F'r soldiers, we answered,—me 'nd Jim,—
He havin' his opinyin uv me,
'Nd I havin' my opinyin uv him.

But down in Tennessee one night
Ther wuz sound uv firin' fur away,
'Nd the sergeant allowed ther 'd be a fight
With the Johnnie Rebs some time nex' day;
'Nd as I wuz thinkin' uv Lizzie 'nd home
Jim stood afore me, long nd 'slim,—
He havin' his opinyin uv me,
'Nd I havin' my opinyin uv him.

Seemed like we knew there wuz goin' to be
Serious trouble f'r me 'nd him;
Us two shuck hands, did Jim 'nd me,
But never a word from me or Jim!
He went his way 'nd I went mine,
'Nd into the battle's roar went we,—
I havin' my opinyin uv Jim,
'Nd he havin' his opinyin uv me.

Jim never come back from the war again,
But I haint forgot that last, last night
When, waitin' f'r orders, us two men
Made up 'nd shuck hands, afore the fight
'Nd, after it all, it's soothin' to know
That here I be 'nd yonder's Jim,—
He havin' his opinyin uv me,
'Nd I havin' my opinyin uv him.

MOTHER AND CHILD.

ONE night a tiny dewdrop fell
Into the bosom of a rose,—
"Dear little one, I love thee well,
Be ever here thy sweet repose!"

Seeing the rose with love bedight,
The envious sky frowned dark, and then
Sent forth a messenger of light
And caught the dewdrop up again.

"Oh, give me back my heavenly child,—
My love!" the rose in anguish cried;
Alas! the sky triumphant smiled,
And so the flower, heart-broken, died.

ORKNEY LULLABY.

A MOONBEAM floateth from the skies,
Whispering, "Heigho, my dearie!
I would spin a web before your eyes,—

A beautiful web of silver light,
Wherein is many a wondrous sight
Of a radiant garden leagues away,
Where the softly tinkling lilies sway,
And the snow-white lambkins are at play,—
Heigho, my dearie!"

A brownie stealeth from the vine
Singing, "Heigho, my dearie!
And will you hear this song of mine,—
A song of the land of murk and mist
Where bideth the bud the dew hath kisst?
Then let the moonbeam's web of light
Be spun before thee silvery white,
And I shall sing the livelong night,—
Heigho, my dearie!"

The night wind speedeth from the sea,
Murmuring, "Heigho, my dearie!
I bring a mariner's prayer for thee;
So let the moonbeam veil thine eyes,
And the brownie sing thee lullabies;
But I shall rock thee to and fro,
Kissing the brow he loveth so,
And the prayer shall guard thy bed, I trow,—
Heigho, my dearie!"

LITTLE MACK.

THIS talk about the journalists that run the East is bosh,
We've got a Western editor that's little, but, O gosh!
He lives here in Mizzoora where the people are so set
In ante-bellum notions that they vote for Jackson yet;

But the paper he is running makes the rusty fossils swear,—
The smartest, likeliest paper that is printed any-where!
And, best of all, the paragraphs are pointed as a tack,
And that's because they emanate
From little Mack.

In architecture he is what you 'd call a chunky man,
As if he 'd been constructed on the summer-cottage plan;

He has a nose like Bonaparte; and round his mobile mouth
Lies all the sensuous languor of the children of the South;
His dealings with reporters who affect a weekly bust
Have given to his violet eyes a shadow of distrust;
In glorious abandon his brown hair wanders back
From the grand Websterian forehead
Of little Mack.

No matter what the item is, if there 's an item in it,
You bet your life he's on to it and nips it in a minute!
From multifarious nations, countries, monarchies, and lands,
From Afric's sunny fountains and India's coral strands,
From Greenland's icy mountains and Siloam's shady rills,
He gathers in his telegrams, and Houser pays the bills;
What though there be a dearth of news, he has a happy knack
Of scraping up a lot of scoops,
Does little Mack.

And learning? Well he knows the folks of every tribe and age
That ever played a part upon this fleeting human stage;
His intellectual system's so extensive and so greedy
That, when it comes to records, he's a walkin' cyclopedy;
For having studied (and digested) all the books a-goin',
It stands to reason he must know about all's worth a-knowin'!

So when a politician with a record's on the track,
We 're apt to hear some history
From little Mack.

And when a fellow-journalist is broke and needs a twenty,
Who's allus ready to whack up a portion of his
plenty?
Who's allus got a wallet that's as full of sordid gain
As his heart is full of kindness and his head is full of brain?
Whose bowels of compassion will in-va-ri-a-bly move

Their owner to those courtesies which plainly, surely prove
That he's the kind of person that never does go back
On a fellow that's in trouble?
Why, little Mack!

I've heard 'em tell of Dana, and of Bonner, and of Reid,
Of Johnnie Cockerill, who, I'll own, is very smart indeed;
Yet I don't care what their renown or influence may be,
One metropolitan exchange is quite enough for me!
So keep your Danas, Bonners, Reids, your Cockerills, and the rest,
The woods is full of better men all through this woolly West;
For all that sleek, pretentious, Eastern editorial pack
We would n't swap the shadow of Our little Mack!

TO ROBIN GOODFELLOW.

I SEE you, Maister Bawsy-brown,
Through yonder lattice creepin';
You come for cream and to gar me dream,
But you dinna find me sleepin'.
The moonbeam, that upon the floor
Wi' crickets ben a-jinkin',

Now steals away fra' her bonnie play—
Wi' a rosier blie, I 'm thinkin'.

I saw you, Maister Bawsy-brown,
When the blue bells went a-ringin'
For the merrie fays o' the banks an' braes,
And I kenned your bonnie singin';
The gowans gave you honey sweets,
And the posies orr the heather
Dript draughts o' dew for the faery crew
That danct and sang together.

But posie-bloom an' simmer-dew
And ither sweets o' faery
Cud na gae down wi' Bawsy-brown,
Sae nigh to Maggie's dairy!
My pantry shelves, sae clean and white,
Are set wi' cream and cheeses,—
Gae, gin you will, an' take your fill
Of whatsoever pleases.

Then wave your wand aboon my een
Until they close awearie,
And the night be past sae sweet and fast
Wi' dreamings o' my dearie.
But pinch the wench in yonder room,
For she's na gude nor bonnie,—
Her shelves be dust and her pans be rust,
And she winkit at my Johnnie!

APPLE-PIE AND CHEESE.

FULL many a sinful notion

Conceived of foreign powers
Has come across the ocean
To harm this land of ours;
And heresies called fashions
Have modesty effaced,
And baleful, morbid passions
Corrupt our native taste.
O tempora! O mores!
What profanations these
That seek to dim the glories
Of apple-pie and cheese!

I'm glad my education
Enables me to stand
Against the vile temptation
Held out on every hand;
Eschewing all the tittles
With vanity replete,

I'm loyal to the victuals
Our grandsires used to eat!
I'm glad I've got three willing boys
To hang around and tease
Their mother for the filling joys
Of apple-pie and cheese!

Your flavored creams and ices
And your dainty angel-food
Are mighty fine devices
To regale the dainty dude;
Your terrapin and oysters,
With wine to wash 'em down,
Are just the thing for roisters

When painting of the town;
No flippant, sugared notion
Shall my appetite appease,
Or bate my soul's devotion
To apple-pie and cheese!

The pie my Julia makes me
(God bless her Yankee ways!)
On memory's pinions takes me
To dear Green Mountain days;

And seems like I saw Mother
Lean on the window-sill,
A-handin' me and brother
What she knows 'll keep us still;
And these feelings are so grateful,
Says I, "Julia, if you please,
I'll take another plateful
Of that apple-pie and cheese!"

And cheese I No alien it, sir,
That's brought across the sea,—
No Dutch antique, nor Switzer,
Nor glutinous de Brie;
There's nothing I abhor so
As mawmets of this ilk—
Give me the harmless morceau
That's made of true-blue milk!
No matter what conditions
Dyspeptic come to feaze,
The best of all physicians
Is apple-pie and cheese!

Though ribalds may decry 'em,
For these twin boons we stand,
Partaking thrice per diem
Of their fulness out of hand;

No enervating fashion
Shall cheat us of our right
To gratify our passion
With a mouthful at a bite!
We 'll cut it square or bias,
Or any way we please,
And faith shall justify us
When we carve our pie and cheese!

De gustibus, 't is stated,
Non disputandum est
Which meaneth, when translated,
That all is for the best
So let the foolish choose 'em
The vapid sweets of sin,
I will not disabuse 'em
Of the heresy they 're in;
But I, when I undress me
Each night, upon my knees
Will ask the Lord to bless me
With apple-pie and cheese!

KRINKEN.

KRINKEN was a little child,—
It was summer when he smiled.
Oft the hoary sea and grim
Stretched its white arms out to him,

Calling, "Sun-child, come to me;
Let me warm my heart with thee!"
But the child heard not the sea,
Calling, yearning evermore
For the summer on the shore.

Krinken on the beach one day
Saw a maiden Nis at play;
On the pebbly beach she played
In the summer Krinken made.
Fair, and very fair, was she,
Just a little child was he.

" Krinken," said the maiden Nis,
"Let me have a little kiss,—
Just a kiss, and go with me
To the summer-lands that be
Down within the silver sea."

Krinken was a little child—
By the maiden Nis beguiled,
Hand in hand with her went he,
And 't was summer in the sea.
And the hoary sea and grim
To its bosom folded him—
Clasped and kissed the little form,
And the ocean's heart was warm.

Now the sea calls out no more; It is winter on the shore,—
Winter where that little child
Made sweet summer when he smiled;
Though 't is summer on the sea
Where with maiden Nis went he,—

Summer, summer evermore,—
It is winter on the shore,
Winter, winter evermore.

Of the summer on the deep
Come sweet visions in my sleep:
His fair face lifts from the sea,
His dear voice calls out to me,—
These my dreams of summer be.

Krinken was a little child,
By the maiden Nis beguiled;
Oft the hoary sea and grim
Reached its longing arms to him,
Crying, "Sun-child, come to me;
Let me warm my heart with thee!"
But the sea calls out no more;
It is winter on the shore,—
Winter, cold and dark and wild;
Krinken was a little child,—
It was summer when he smiled;
Down he went into the sea,
And the winter bides with me.
Just a little child was he.

BERANGER'S "BROKEN FIDDLE"

I.

THERE, there, poor dog, my faithful friend,
Pay you no heed unto my sorrow:
But feast to-day while yet you may,—
Who knows but we shall starve to-morrow!

II.

"Give us a tune," the foemen cried,
In one of their profane caprices;
I bade them "No "—they frowned, and, lo!
They dashed this innocent in pieces!

III.

This fiddle was the village pride—
The mirth of every fête enhancing;
Its wizard art set every heart
As well as every foot to dancing.

IV.

How well the bridegroom knew its voice,
As from its strings its song went gushing!
Nor long delayed the promised maid
Equipped for bridal, coy and blushing.

V.

Why, it discoursed so merrily,
It quickly banished all dejection;
And yet, when pressed, our priest confessed
I played with pious circumspection.

VI.

And though, in patriotic song,
It was our guide, compatriot, teacher,
I never thought the foe had wrought

His fury on the helpless creature!

VII.

But there, poor dog, my faithful friend,
Pay you no heed unto my sorrow;
I prithee take this paltry cake,—
Who knows but we shall starve to-morrow!

VIII.

Ah, who shall lead the Sunday choir
As this old fiddle used to do it?
Can vintage come, with this voice dumb
That used to bid a welcome to it?

IX.

It soothed the weary hours of toil,
It brought forgetfulness to debtors;
Time and again from wretched men
It struck oppression's galling fetters.

X.

No man could hear its voice, and hate;
It stayed the teardrop at its portal;
With that dear thing I was a king
As never yet was monarch mortal!

XI.

Now has the foe—the vandal foe—

Struck from my hands their pride and glory;
There let it lie! In vengeance, I
Shall wield another weapon, gory!

And if, O countrymen, I fall,
Beside our grave let this be spoken:
"No foe of France shall ever dance
Above the heart and fiddle, broken!"

XIII.

So come, poor dog, my faithful friend,
I prithee do not heed my sorrow,
But feast to-day while yet you may,
For we are like to starve to-morrow.

THE LITTLE PEACH.

A LITTLE peach in the orchard grew,—
A little peach of emerald hue;
Warmed by the sun and wet by the dew, It grew.

One day, passing that orchard through,
That little peach dawned on the view
Of Johnny Jones and his sister Sue—
Them two.

Up at that peach a club they threw—
Down from the stem on which it grew
Fell that peach of emerald hue.
Mon Dieu!

John took a bite and Sue a chew,

And then the trouble began to brew,—
Trouble the doctor could n't subdue.
Too true!

Under the turf where the daisies grew
' They planted John and his sister Sue,
And their little souls to the angels flew,—
Boo hoo!

What of that peach of the emerald hue,
Warmed by the sun, and wet by the dew?
Ah, well, its mission on earth is through.
Adieu!
1880.

HORACE III. 13.

O FOUNTAIN of Bandusia,
Whence crystal waters flow,
With garlands gay and wine I'll pay
The sacrifice I owe;
A sportive kid with budding horns
I have, whose crimson blood
Anon shall dye and sanctify
Thy cool and babbling flood.

O fountain of Bandusia,
The dogstar's hateful spell
No evil brings unto the springs
That from thy bosom well;
Here oxen, wearied by the plough,
The roving cattle here,
Hasten in quest of certain rest

And quaff thy gracious cheer.

O fountain of Bandusia,
Ennobled shalt thou be,
For I shall sing the joys that spring
Beneath yon ilex-tree;
Yes, fountain of Bandusia,
Posterity shall know
The cooling brooks that from thy nooks
Singing and dancing go!

THE DIVINE LULLABY.

I HEAR Thy voice, dear Lord;
I hear it by the stormy sea
When winter nights are black and wild,
And when, affright, I call to Thee;
It calms my fears and whispers me,
"Sleep well, my child."

I hear Thy voice, dear Lord,
In singing winds, in falling snow,
The curfew chimes, the midnight bell,
"Sleep well, my child," it murmurs low;
"The guardian angels come and go,—
O child, sleep well!"

I hear Thy voice, dear Lord,
Ay, though the singing winds be stilled,
Though hushed the tumult of the deep,
My fainting heart with anguish chilled
By Thy assuring tone is thrilled,—
"Fear not, and sleep!"

Speak on—speak on, dear Lord!
And when the last dread night is near,
With doubts and fears and terrors wild,
Oh, let my soul expiring hear
Only these words of heavenly cheer,
"Sleep well, my child!"

Oh, for an hour in that dear place!
Oh, for the peace of that dear time!
Oh, for that childish trust sublime!
Oh, for a glimpse of Mother's face!
Yet, as the shadows round me creep,
I do not seem to be alone,—
Sweet magic of that treble tone,
And "Now I lay me down to sleep."

1885.

HEINE'S "WIDOW OR DAUGHTER?

SHALL I woo the one or other?
Both attract me—more's the pity!
Pretty is the widowed mother,
And the daughter, too, is pretty.

When I see that maiden shrinking,
By the gods I swear I'll get 'er!
But anon I fall to thinking
That the mother 'll suit me better!

So, like any idiot ass
Hungry for the fragrant fodder,

Placed between two bales of grass,
Lo, I doubt, delay, and dodder!

CHRISTMAS TREASURES.

I COUNT my treasures o'er with care,—
The little toy my darling knew,
A little sock of faded hue,
A little lock of golden hair.

Long years ago this holy time,
My little one—my all to me—
Sat robed in white upon my knee
And heard the merry Christmas chime.

"Tell me, my little golden-head,
If Santa Claus should come to-night,
What shall he bring my baby bright,—
What treasure for my boy?" I said.

And then he named this little toy,
While in his round and mournful eyes
There came a look of sweet surprise,
That spake his quiet, trustful joy.

And as he lisped his evening prayer
He asked the boon with childish grace;
Then, toddling to the chimney-place,
He hung this little stocking there.

That night, while lengthening shadows crept,
I saw the white-winged angels come
With singing to our lowly home

And kiss my darling as he slept

They must have heard his little prayer,
For in the morn, with rapturous face,
He toddled to the chimney-place,
And found this little treasure there.

They came again one Christmas-tide,—
That angel host, so fair and white!
And singing all that glorious night,
They lured my darling from my side.

A little sock, a little toy,
A little lock of golden hair,
The Christmas music on the air,
A watching for my baby boy!

But if again that angel train
And golden-head come back for me,
To bear me to Eternity,
My watching will not be in vain!

1879.

DE AMICITIIS.

Though care and strife
Elsewhere be rife,
Upon my word I do not heed 'em;
In bed I lie
With books hard by,
And with increasing zest I read 'em.

Propped up in bed,
So much I 've read
Of musty tomes that I 've a headful
Of tales and rhymes
Of ancient times,
Which, wife declares, are "Simply dreadful!"

They give me joy
Without alloy;
And is n't that what books are made for?
And yet—and yet—
(Ah, vain regret!)
I would to God they all were paid for!

No festooned cup
Filled foaming up
Can lure me elsewhere to confound me;
Sweeter than wine
This love of mine
For these old books I see around me!

A plague, I say,
On maidens gay;
I'll weave no compliments to tell 'em!
Vain fool I were,
Did I prefer
Those dolls to these old friends in vellum!

At dead of night
My chamber's bright
Not only with the gas that's burning,
But with the glow
Of long ago,—

Of beauty back from eld returning.

Fair women's looks
I see in books,
I see them, and I hear their laughter,—
Proud, high-born maids,
Unlike the jades
Which menfolk now go chasing after!

Herein again
Speak valiant men
Of all nativities and ages;
I hear and smile
With rapture while
I turn these musty, magic pages.

The sword, the lance,
The morris dance,
The highland song, the greenwood ditty,
Of these I read,
Or, when the need,
My Miller grinds me grist that's gritty!

When of such stuff
We 've had enough,
Why, there be other friends to greet us;
We 'll moralize
In solemn wise
With Plato or with Epictetus.

Sneer as you may,
I'm proud to say
That I, for one, am very grateful

To Heaven, that sends
These genial friends
To banish other friendships hateful!

And when I 'm done,
I 'd have no son
Pounce on these treasures like a vulture;
Nay, give them half
My epitaph,
And let them share in my sepulture.

Then, when the crack
Of doom rolls back
The marble and the earth that hide me,
I'll smuggle home
Each precious tome,
Without a fear my wife shall chide me!

OUR LADY OF THE MINE.

THE Blue Horizon wuz a mine us fellers all thought well uv,
And there befell the episode I now perpose to tell uv;
'T wuz in the year uv sixty-nine,—somewhere along in summer,—
There hove in sight one afternoon a new and curious comer;
His name wuz Silas Pettibone,—a artist by perfession,—
With a kit of tools and a big mustache and a pipe in his possession.
He told us, by our leave, he 'd kind uv like to make some sketches
Uv the snowy peaks, 'nd the foamin' crick, 'nd the distant mountain stretches;
"You 're welkim, sir," sez we, although this scenery dodge seemed to us
A waste uv time where scenery wuz already sooperfloo-us.

All through the summer Pettibone kep' busy at his sketching',—
At daybreak off for Eagle Pass, and home at nightfall, fetchin'

That everlastin' book uv his with spider-lines all through it;
Three-Fingered Hoover used to say there warn't no meanin' to it
"Gol durn a man," sez he to him, " whose shif'less hand is sot at
A-drawin' hills that 's full uv quartz that's pinin' to be got at!"
"Go on," sez Pettibone, "go on, if joshin' gratifies ye;
But one uv these fine times I'll show ye sumthin' will surprise ye!"
The which remark led us to think—although he didn't say it—
That Pettibone wuz owin' us a gredge 'nd meant to pay it

One evenin' as we sat around the Restauraw de Casey,
A-singin' songs 'nd tellin' yarns the which wuz
sumwhat racy,

In come that feller Pettibone, 'nd sez, " With your permission,
I 'd like to put a picture I have made on exhibition."
He sot the picture on the bar 'nd drew aside its curtain,
Sayin', "I recken you 'll allow as how that's art, f'r certain!"
And then we looked, with jaws agape, but nary word wuz spoken,
And f'r a likely spell the charm uv silence wuz unbroken—
Till presently, as in a dream, remarked Three-Fingered Hoover:
"Onless I am mistaken, this is Pettibone's shef doover!"

It wuz a face—a human face—a woman's, fair 'nd tender—
Sot gracefully upon a neck white as a swan's, and slender;
The hair wuz kind uv sunny, 'nd the eyes wuz sort uv dreamy,
The mouth wuz half a-smilin', 'nd the cheeks wuz soft 'nd creamy;

It seemed like she wuz lookin' off into the west out yonder,
And seemed like, while she looked, we saw her eyes grow softer, fonder,—
Like, lookin' off into the west, where mountain mists wuz fallin',
She saw the face she longed to see and heerd his voice a-callin';
"Hooray!" we cried,—"a woman in the camp uv Blue Horizon!
Step right up, Colonel Pettibone, 'nd nominate your pizen!"

A curious situation,—one deservin' uv your pity,—
No human, livin', female thing this side of Denver City!
But jest a lot uv husky men that lived on sand 'nd bitters,—
Do you wonder that that woman's face consoled the lonesome critters?
And not a one but what it served in some way to remind him
Of a mother or a sister or a sweetheart left behind him;

And some looked back on happier days, and saw the old-time faces
And heerd the dear familiar sounds in old familiar places,—
A gracious touch of home. "Look here," sez Hoover, "ever'body
Quit thinkin' 'nd perceed at oncet to name his favorite toddy!"

It wuz n't long afore the news had spread the country over,
And miners come a-flockin' in like honey-bees to clover;
It kind uv did 'em good, they said, to feast their hungry eyes on
That picture uv Our Lady in the camp uv Blue Horizon.
But one mean cuss from Nigger Crick passed criticisms on 'er,—
Leastwise we overheerd him call her Pettibone's madonner,
The which we did not take to be respectful to a lady,
So we hung him in a quiet spot that wuz cool 'nd dry 'nd shady;

Which same might not have been good law, but it wuz the right maneuver
To give the critics due respect for Pettibone's shef doover.

Gone is the camp,—yes, years ago the Blue Horizon busted,
And every mother's son uv us got up one day 'nd dusted,
While Pettibone perceeded East with wealth in his possession,
And went to Yurrup, as I heerd, to study his perfession;
So, like as not, you 'll find him now a-paintin' heads 'nd faces
At Venus, Billy Florence, and the like I-talyun places.
But no sech face he 'll paint again as at old Blue Horizon,
For I'll allow no sweeter face no human soul sot eyes on;

And when the critics talk so grand uv Paris 'nd the Loover,
I say, " Oh, but you orter seen the Pettibone shef doover!"

THE WANDERER.

UPON a mountain height, far from the sea,
 I found a shell,
And to my listening ear the lonely thing
Ever a song of ocean seemed to sing,
Ever a tale of ocean seemed to tell.

How came the shell upon that mountain height?
Ah, who can say
Whether there dropped by some too careless hand,
Or whether there cast when Ocean swept the Land,
Ere the Eternal had ordained the Day?

Strange, was it not? Far from its native deep,
One song it sang,—
Sang of the awful mysteries of the tide,
Sang of the misty sea, profound and wide,—
Ever with echoes of the ocean rang.

And as the shell upon the mountain height
Sings of the sea,
So do I ever, leagues and leagues away,—
So do I ever, wandering where I may,—
Sing, O my home! sing, O my home! of thee.

1883.

TO A USURPER.

A HA! a traitor in the camp,
A rebel strangely bold,—
A lisping, laughing, toddling scamp,
Not more than four years old!

To think that I, who 've ruled alone
So proudly in the past,
Should be ejected from my throne
By my own son at last!

He trots his treason to and fro,
As only babies can,
And says he 'll be his mamma's beau
When he's a "gweat, big man"!

You stingy boy! you 've always had
A share in mamma's heart;
Would you begrudge your poor old dad
The tiniest little part?

That mamma, I regret to see,
Inclines to take your part,—
As if a dual monarchy
Should rule her gentle heart!

But when the years of youth have sped,
The bearded man, I trow,
Will quite forget he ever said

He 'd be his mamma's beau.

Renounce your treason, little son,
Leave mamma's heart to me;
For there will come another one
To claim your loyalty.

And when that other comes to you,
God grant her love may shine
Through all your life, as fair and true
As mamma's does through mine!

1885

LULLABY; BY THE SEA.

FAIR is the castle up on the hill—
A Hushaby, sweet my own!
The night is fair, and the waves are still,
And the wind is singing to you and to me
In this lowly home beside the sea—
Hushaby, sweet my own!

On yonder hill is store of wealth—
Hushaby, sweet my own!
And revellers drink to a little one's health;
But you and I bide night and day
For the other love that has sailed away—
Hushaby, sweet my own!

See not, dear eyes, the forms that creep
Ghostlike, O my own!
Out of the mists of the murmuring deep;

Oh, see them not and make no cry
Till the angels of death have passed us by—
Hushaby, sweet my own!

Ah, little they reck of you and me—
Hushaby, sweet my own!
In our lonely home beside the sea;
They seek the castle up on the hill,
And there they will do their ghostly will—
Hushaby, O my own!

Here by the sea a mother croons
"Hushaby, sweet my own!"
In yonder castle a mother swoons
While the angels go down to the misty deep,
Bearing a little one fast asleep—
Hushaby, sweet my own!

SOLDIER, MAIDEN, AND FLOWER.

"SWEETHEART, take this," a soldier said,
"And bid me brave good-by;
It may befall we ne'er shall wed,
But love can never die.
Be steadfast in thy troth to me,
And then, whate'er my lot,
'My soul to God, my heart to thee,'—
Sweetheart, forget me not!"

The maiden took the tiny flower
And nursed it with her tears:
Lo! he who left her in that hour
Came not in after years.

Unto a hero's death he rode
'Mid shower of fire and shot;
But in the maiden's heart abode
The flower, forget-me-not.

And when he came not with the rest
From out the years of blood,
Closely unto her widowed breast
She pressed a faded bud;
Oh, there is love and there is pain,
And there is peace, God wot,—
And these dear three do live again
In sweet forget-me-not.

'T is to an unmarked grave to-day
That I should love to go,—
Whether he wore the blue or gray,
What need that we should know.
"He loved a woman," let us say,
And on that sacred spot,
To woman's love, that lives for aye,
We 'll strew forget-me-not.

1887.

HORACE TO MELPOMENE.

LOFTY and enduring is the monument I 've reared,—
Come, tempests, with your bitterness assailing;
And thou, corrosive blasts of time, by all things mortal feared,
Thy buffets and thy rage are unavailing!

I shall not altogether die; by far my greater part

Shall mock man's common fate in realms infernal;
My works shall live as tributes to my genius and my art,—
My works shall be my monument eternal!

While this great Roman empire stands and gods protect our fanes,
Mankind with grateful hearts shall tell the story,
How-one most lowly born upon the parched Apulian plains
First raised the native lyric muse to glory.

Assume, revered Melpomene, the proud estate I 've won,
And, with thine own dear hand the meed supplying,
Bind thou about the forehead of thy celebrated son
The Delphic laurel-wreath of fame undying!

AILSIE, MY BAIRN.

THE in my arms, Ailsie, my bairn,—
Lie in my arms and dinna greit;
Long time been past syn I kenned you last,
But my harte been allwais the same, my swete.

Ailsie, I colde not say you ill,
For out of the mist of your bitter tears,
And the prayers that rise from your bonnie eyes
Cometh a promise of oder yeres.

I mind the time when we lost our bairn,—
Do you ken that time? A wambling tot,
You wandered away ane simmer day,
And we hunted and called, and found you not.

I promised God, if He 'd send you back,
Alwaies to keepe and to love you, childe;

And I 'm thinking again of that promise when
I see you creep out of the storm sae wild.

You came back then as you come back now,—
Your kirtle torn and your face all white;
And you stood outside and knockit and cried,
Just as you, dearie, did to-night

Oh, never a word of the cruel wrang,
That has faded your cheek and dimmed your ee;
And never a word of the fause, fause lord,—
Only a smile and a kiss for me.

Lie in my arms, as long, long syne,
And sleepe on my bosom, deere wounded thing,—
I 'm nae sae glee as I use to be,
Or I 'd sing you the songs I use to sing.

But He kemb my fingers thro' yr haire,
And nane shall know, but you and I,
Of the love and the faith that came to us baith
When Ailsie, my bairn, came home to die.

CORNISH LULLABY.

OUT on the mountain over the town,
All night long, all night long,
The trolls go up and the trolls go down,
Bearing their packs and crooning a song;
And this is the song the hill-folk croon,
As they trudge in the light of the misty moon,—
This is ever their dolorous tune:
"Gold, gold! ever more gold,—

Bright red gold for dearie!"

Deep in the hill the yeoman delves
All night long, all night long;
None but the peering, furtive elves
See his toil and hear his song;
Merrily ever the cavern rings
As merrily ever his pick he swings,
And merrily ever this song he sings:
"Gold, gold! ever more gold,—
Bright red gold for dearie!"

Mother is rocking thy lowly bed
All night long, all night long,
Happy to smooth thy curly head
And to hold thy hand and to sing her song;
'T is not of the hill-folk, dwarfed and old,
Nor the song of the yeoman, stanch and bold,
And the burden it beareth is not of gold;
But it's "love, love I—nothing but love,—
Mother's love for dearie!"

UHLAND'S "THREE CAVALIERS."
THERE were three cavaliers that went over the Rhine,
And gayly they called to the hostess for wine.
"And where is thy daughter? We would she were here,—
Go fetch us that maiden to gladden our cheer!"

"I'll fetch thee thy goblets full foaming," she said,
"But in yon darkened chamber the maiden lies dead."
And lo! as they stood in the doorway, the white
Of a shroud and a dead shrunken face met their sight.

Then the first cavalier breathed a pitiful sigh,
And the throb of his heart seemed to melt in his eye,

And he cried, "Hadst thou lived, O my pretty white rose,
I ween I had loved thee and wed thee—who knows?"

The next cavalier drew aside a small space,
And stood to the wall with his hands to his face;
And this was the heart-cry that came with his tears:
" I loved her, I loved her these many long years!"

But the third cavalier kneeled him down in that place,
And, as it were holy, he kissed that dead face:
" I loved thee long years, and I love thee to-day,
And I'll love thee, dear maiden, forever and aye!"

A CHAUCERIAN PARAPHRASE OF HORACE.

SYN that you, Chloe, to your moder sticken,
Maketh all ye yonge bacheloures full sicken;
Like as a lyttel deere you ben y-hiding
Whenas come lovers with theyre pityse chiding;
Sothly it ben faire to give up your moder
For to beare swete company with some oder;
Your moder ben well enow so farre shee goeth,
But that ben not farre enow, God knoweth;
Wherefore it ben sayed that foolysh ladyes
That marrye not shall leade an aype in Hadys;
But all that do with gode men wed full quickylye
When that they be on dead go to ye seints full sickerly.

NORSE LULLABY.

THE sky is dark and the hills are white
As the storm-king speeds from the north to-night,
And this is the song the storm-king sings,
As over the world his cloak he flings:
"Sleep, sleep, little one, sleep;"
He rustles his wings and gruffly sings:
"Sleep, little one, sleep."

On yonder mountain-side a vine
Clings at the foot of a mother pine;
The tree bends over the trembling thing,
And only the vine can hear her sing:
"Sleep, sleep, little one, sleep;
What shall you fear when I am here?
Sleep, little one, sleep."

The king may sing in his bitter flight,
The tree may croon to the vine to-night,
But the little snowflake at my breast
Liketh the song I sing the best,—
Sleep, sleep, little one, sleep;
Weary thou art, anext my heart
Sleep, little one, sleep.

BÉRANGER'S "MY LAST SONG PERHAPS."

[January, 1814.]

WHEN, to despoil my native France,

With flaming torch and cruel sword
And boisterous drums her foeman comes,
I curse him and his vandal horde!
Yet, what avail accrues to her,
If we assume the garb of woe?
Let's merry be,—in laughter we
May rescue somewhat from the foe!

Ah, many a brave man trembles now.
I (coward!) show no sign of fear;
When Bacchus sends his blessing, friends,
I drown my panic in his cheer.
Come, gather round my humble board,
And let the sparkling wassail flow,—
Chuckling to think, the while you drink,
"This much we rescue from the foe!"

My creditors beset me so
And so environed my abode,
That I agreed, despite my need,
To settle up the debts I owed;
When suddenly there came the news
Of this invasion, as you know;
I'll pay no score; pray, lend me more,—
I—I will keep it from the foe!

Now here 's my mistress,—pretty dear!—
Feigns terror at this martial noise,
And yet, methinks, the artful minx
Would like to meet those soldier boys!
I tell her that they 're coarse and rude,
Yet feel she don't believe 'em so,—
Well, never mind; so she be kind,

That much I rescue from the foe!

If, brothers, hope shall have in store
For us and ours no friendly glance,
Let's rather die than raise a cry
Of welcome to the foes of France!
But, like the swan that dying sings,
Let us, O Frenchmen, singing go,—
Then shall our cheer, when death is near,
Be so much rescued from the foe!

MR. DANA, OF THE NEW YORK SUN.

THAR showed up out 'n Denver in the spring uv '81
A man who 'd worked with Dana on the Noo York Sun.
His name wuz Cantell Whoppers, 'nd he wuz a sight ter view
Ez he walked inter the orfice 'nd inquired fer work to do.
Thar warn't no places vacant then,—fer be it understood,
That wuz the time when talent flourished at that altitood;
But thar the stranger lingered, tellin' Raymond 'nd the rest
Uv what perdigious wonders he could do when at his best,
'Til finally he stated (quite by chance) that he hed done
A heap uv work with Dana on the Noo York Sun.

Wall, that wuz quite another thing; we owned that ary cuss
Who 'd worked f r Mr. Dana must be good enough fer us!
And so we tuk the stranger's word 'nd nipped him while we could,
For if we didn't take him we knew John Arkins would;
And Cooper, too, wuz mouzin' round fer enterprise 'nd brains,
Whenever them commodities blew in across the plains.
At any rate we nailed him, which made ol' Cooper swear
And Arkins tear out handfuls uv his copious curly hair;
But we set back and cackled, 'nd hed a power uv fun

With our man who 'd worked with Dana on the Noo York Sun.
It made our eyes hang on our cheeks 'nd lower jaws ter drop,
Ter hear that feller tellin' how ol' Dana run his shop:

It seems that Dana wuz the biggest man you ever saw,—
He lived on human bein's, 'nd preferred to eat 'em raw!
If he hed democratic drugs ter take, before he took em',
As good old allopathic laws prescribe, he allus shook 'em.
The man that could set down 'nd write like Dany never grew,
And the sum of human knowledge wuz n't half what Dana knew;
The consequence appeared to be that nearly every one
Concurred with Mr. Dana of the Noo York Sun.

This feller, Cantell Whoppers, never brought an item in,—
He spent his time at Perrin's shakin' poker dice f'r gin.
Whatever the assignment he wuz allus sure to shirk,
He wuz very long on likker and all-fired short on work!
If any other cuss had played the tricks he dared ter play,

The daisies would be bloomin' over his remains to-day;
But somehow folks respected him and stood him to the last,
Considerin' his superior connections in the past.
So, when he bilked at poker, not a sucker drew a gun
On the man who 'd worked with Dana on the Noo York Sun.

Wall, Dana came ter Denver in the fall uv '83,
A very different party from the man we thought ter see,—
A nice 'nd clean old gentleman, so dignerfied 'nd calm,
You bet yer life he never did no human bein' harm!
A certain hearty manner 'nd a fulness uv the vest
Betokened that his sperrits 'nd his victuals wuz the best;
His face was so benevolent, his smile so sweet 'nd kind,
That they seemed to be the reflex uv an honest, healthy mind;

And God had set upon his head a crown uv silver hair

In promise uv the golden crown He meaneth him to wear.
So, uv us boys that met him out *n Denver, there wuz none
But fell in love with Dana uv the Noo York Sun.

But when he came to Denver in that fall uv '83,
His old friend Cantell Whoppers disappeared upon a spree;
The very thought uv seein' Dana worked upon him so
(They had n't been together fer a year or two, you know),
That he borrered all the stuff he could and started on a bat,
And, strange as it may seem, we did n't see him after that.
So, when ol' Dana hove in sight, we could n't understand
Why he didn't seem to notice that his crony wa' n't on hand;
No casual allusion, not a question, no, not one,
For the man who 'd " worked with Dana on the Noo York Sun!"

We broke it gently to him, but he didn't seem surprised,
Thar wuz no big burst uv passion as we fellers had surmised.
He said that Whoppers wuz a man he'd never heerd about,
But he mought have carried papers on a Jarsey City route;
And then he recollected hearin' Mr. Laffan say
That he 'd fired a man named Whoppers fur bein' drunk one day,
Which, with more likker underneath than money in his vest,
Had started on a freight train fur the great 'nd boundin' West,
But further information or statistics he had none
Uv the man who 'd " worked with Dana on the Noo York Sun."

We dropped the matter quietly 'nd never made no fuss,—
When we get played for suckers, why, that's a horse on us!—
But every now 'nd then we Denver fellers have to laff

To hear some other paper boast uv havin' on its staff

A man who's "worked with Dana," 'nd then we fellers wink
And pull our hats down on our eyes 'nd set around 'nd think.
It seems like Dana couldn't be as smart as people say,
If he educates so many folks 'nd lets 'em get away;
And, as for us, in future we'll be very apt to shun
The man who "worked with Dana on the Noo York Sun."

But bless ye, Mr. Dana! may you live a thousan' years,
To sort o' keep things lively in this vale of human tears;
An' may I live a thousan', too,—a thousan' less a day,
For I should n't like to be on earth to hear you 'd passed away.
And when it comes your time to go you 'll need no Latin chaff

Nor biographic data put in your epitaph;
But one straight line of English and of truth will let folks know
The homage 'nd the gratitude 'nd reverence they owe;
You'll need no epitaph but this: "Here sleeps the man who run
That best 'nd brightest paper, the Noo York Sun."

SICILIAN LULLABY.

HUSH, little one; and fold your hands;
The sun hath set, the moon is high;
The sea is singing to the sands,
And wakeful posies are beguiled
By many a fairy lullaby:
Hush, little child, my little child!

Dream, little one, and in your dreams
Float upward from this lowly place,—
Float out on mellow, misty streams
To lands where bideth Mary mild,
And let her kiss thy little face,

You little child, my little child!

Sleep, little one, and take thy rest,
With angels bending over thee,—
Sleep sweetly on that Father's breast
Whom our dear Christ hath reconciled;
But stay not there,—come back to me,
O little child, my little child!

HORACE TO PYRRHA.

WHAT perfumed, posie-dizened sirrah,
** With smiles for diet,
Clasps you, O fair but faithless Pyrrha, On the quiet?
For whom do you bind up your tresses,
As spun-gold yellow,—
Meshes that go, with your caresses,
To snare a fellow?

How will he rail at fate capricious,
And curse you duly!
Yet now he deems your wiles delicious,
You perfect, truly!
Pyrrha, your love's a treacherous ocean;
He 'll soon fall in there!
Then shall I gloat on his commotion,
For I have been there!

THE TWENTY-THIRD PSALM.

MY Shepherd is the Lord my God,—
There is no want I know;
His flock He leads in verdant meads,

Where tranquil waters flow.

He doth restore my fainting soul
With His divine caress,
And, when I stray, He points the way
To paths of righteousness.

Yea, though I walk the vale of death,
What evil shall I fear?
Thy staff and rod are mine, O God,
And Thou, my Shepherd, near!

Mine enemies behold the feast
Which my dear Lord hath spread;
And, lo! my cup He filleth up,
With oil anoints my head!

Goodness and mercy shall be mine
Unto my dying day;
Then will I bide at His dear side
Forever and for aye!

THE BIBLIOMANIACS BRIDE.

TE womenfolk are like to books,—
Most pleasing to the eye,
Whereon if anybody looks
He feels disposed to buy.

I hear that many are for sale,—
Those that record no dates,
And such editions as regale
The view with colored plates.

Of every quality and grade
And size they may be found,—
Quite often beautifully made,
As often poorly bound.

Now, as for me, had I my choice,
I ' choose no folio tall,
But some octavo to rejoice
My sight and heart withal,—

As plump and pudgy as a snipe;
Well worth her weight in gold;
Of honest, clean, conspicuous type,
And just the size to hold!

With such a volume for my wife,
How should I keep and con!
How like a dream should run my life
Unto its colophon!

Her frontispiece should be more fair
Than any colored plate;
Blooming with health, she would not care
To extra-illustrate.

And in her pages there should be
A wealth of prose and verse,
With now and then a jeu d'esprit,—
But nothing ever worse!

Prose for me when I wished for prose,
Verse when to verse inclined,—

Forever bringing sweet repose
To body, heart, and mind.

Oh, I should bind this priceless prize
In bindings full and fine,
And keep her where no human eyes
Should see her charms, but mine!

With such a fair unique as this
What happiness abounds!
Who—who could paint my rapturous bliss,
My joy unknown to Lowndes!

CHRISTMAS HYMN.

Sing, Christmas bells!
Say to the earth this is the morn
Whereon our Saviour-King is born;
Sing to all men,—the bond, the free,
The rich, the poor, the high, the low,
The little child that sports in glee,
The aged folk that tottering go,—
Proclaim the morn
That Christ is born,
That saveth them and saveth me!

Sing, angel host!
Sing of the star that God has placed
Above the manger in the east;
Sing of the glories of the night,
The virgin's sweet humility,
The Babe with kingly robes bedight,—
Sing to all men where'er they be

This Christmas morn;
For Christ is born,
That saveth them and saveth me!

Sing, sons of earth!
O ransomed seed of Adam, sing!
God liveth, and we have a king!
The curse is gone, the bond are free,—
By Bethlehem's star that brightly beamed,
By all the heavenly signs that be,
We know that Israel is redeemed;
That on this morn
The Christ is born
That saveth you and saveth me!

Sing, O my heart!
Sing thou in rapture this dear morn
Whereon the blessed Prince is born!
And as thy songs shall be of love,
So let my deeds be charity,—
By the dear Lord that reigns above,
By Him that died upon the tree,
By this fair morn
Whereon is born
The Christ that saveth all and me!

JAPANESE LULLABY.

SLEEP, little pigeon, and fold your wings,—
Little blue pigeon with velvet eyes;
Sleep to the singing of mother-bird swinging—
Swinging the nest where her little one lies.

Away out yonder I see a star,—
Silvery star with a tinkling song;
To the soft dew falling I hear it calling—
Calling and tinkling the night along.

In through the window a moonbeam comes,—
Little gold moonbeam with misty wings;
All silently creeping, it asks, "Is he sleeping—
Sleeping and dreaming while mother sings?"

Up from the sea there floats the sob
Of the waves that are breaking upon the shore,
As though they were groaning in anguish, and moaning—
Bemoaning the ship that shall come no more.

But sleep, little pigeon, and fold your wings,—
Little blue pigeon with mournful eyes;
Am I not singing?—see, I am swinging—
Swinging the nest where my darling lies.

"GOOD-BY—GOD BLESS YOU!"

I LIKE the Anglo-Saxon speech
With its direct revealings;
It takes a hold, and seems to reach
Way down into your feelings;
That some folk deem it rude, I know,
And therefore they abuse it;
But I have never found it so,—
Before all else I choose it.
I don't object that men should air
The Gallic they have paid for,
With "Au revqir," "Adieu, ma chere,"

For that's what French was made for.
But when a crony takes your hand
At parting, to address you,
He drops all foreign lingo and
He says, "Good-by—God bless you!"

This seems to me a sacred phrase,
With reverence impassioned,—
A thing come down from righteous days,
Quaintly but nobly fashioned;
It well becomes an honest face,
A voice that's round and cheerful;
It stays the sturdy in his place,
And soothes the weak and fearful.
Into the porches of the ears
It steals with subtle unction,
And in your heart of hearts appears
To work its gracious function;
And all day long with pleasing song
It lingers to caress you,—
I 'm sure no human heart goes wrong
That's told u Good-by—God bless you!"

I love the words,—perhaps because,
When I was leaving Mother,
Standing at last in solemn pause
We looked at one another,
And I—I saw in Mother's eyes
The love she could not tell me,—
A love eternal as the skies,
Whatever fate befell me;
She put her arms about my neck
And soothed the pain of leaving,

And though her heart was like to break,
She spoke no word of grieving;
She let no tear bedim her eye,
For fear that might distress me,
But, kissing me, she said good-by,
And asked our God to bless me.

HORACE TO PHYLLIS.

COME, Phyllis, I 've a cask of wine
That fairly reeks with precious juices,
And in your tresses you shall twine
The loveliest flowers this vale produces.

My cottage wears a gracious smile,—
The altar, decked in floral glory,
Yearns for the lamb which bleats the while
As though it pined for honors gory.

Hither our neighbors nimbly fare,—
The boys agog, the maidens snickering;
And savory smells possess the air
As skyward kitchen flames are flickering.

You ask what means this grand display,
This festive throng, and goodly diet?
Well, since you 're bound to have your way,
I don't mind telling, on the quiet.

'T is April 13, as you know,—
A day and month devote to Venus,
Whereon was born, some years ago,

My very worthy friend Maecenas.

Nay, pay no heed to Telephus,—
Your friends agree he does n't love you;
The way he flirts convinces us
He really is not worthy of you!

Aurora's son, unhappy lad!
You know the fate that overtook him?
And Pegasus a rider had—
I say he had before he shook him!

Haec docet (as you must agree):
'T is meet that Phyllis should discover
A wisdom in preferring me
And mittening every other lover.

So come, O Phyllis, last and best
Of loves with which this heart's been smitten,—
Come, sing my jealous fears to rest,
And let your songs be those I've written.

CHRYSTMASSE OF OLDE.

GOD rest you, Chrysten gentil men,
Wherever you may be,—
God rest you all in fielde or hall,
Or on ye stormy sea;
For on this morn oure Chryst is born
That saveth you and me.

Last night ye shepherds in ye east
Saw many a wondrous thing;

Ye sky last night flamed passing bright
Whiles that ye stars did sing,
And angels came to bless ye name
Of Jesus Chryst, oure Kyng.

God rest you, Chrysten gentil men,
Faring where'er you may;
In noblesse court do thou no sport,
In tournament no playe,
In paynim lands hold thou thy hands
From bloudy works this daye.

But thinking on ye gentil Lord
That died upon ye tree,
Let troublings cease and deeds of peace
Abound in Chrystantie;
For on this morn ye Chryst is born
That saveth you and me.

AT THE DOOR.

I THOUGHT myself indeed secure,
So fast the door, so firm the lock;
But, lo! he toddling comes to lure
My parent ear with timorous knock.

My heart were stone could it withstand
The sweetness of my baby's plea,—
That timorous, baby knocking and
"Please let me in,"—it's only me."

I threw aside the unfinished book,
Regardless of its tempting charms,

And opening wide the door, I took
My laughing darling in my arms.

Who knows but in Eternity,
I, like a truant child, shall wait
The glories of a life to be,
Beyond the Heavenly Father's gate?

And will that Heavenly Father heed
The truant's supplicating cry,
As at the outer door I plead,
" 'T is I, O Father! only I?"

1886.

HI-SPY.

STRANGE that the city thoroughfare,
Noisy and bustling all the day,
Should with the night renounce its care
And lend itself to children's play!

Oh, girls are girls, and boys are boys,
And have been so since Abel's birth,
And shall be so 'til dolls and toys
Are with the children swept from earth.

The self-same sport that crowns the day
Of many a Syrian shepherd's son,
Beguiles the little lads at play
By night in stately Babylon.

I hear their voices in the street,

Yet 't is so different now from then!
Come, brother! from your winding sheet,
And let us two be boys again!

1886.

LITTLE CROODLIN DOO.

HO, pretty bee, did you see my croodlin doo?
Ho, little lamb, is she jinkin' on the lea?
Ho, bonnie fairy, bring my dearie back to me—
Got a lump o' sugar an' a posie for you,
Only bring back my wee, wee croodlin doo!

Why, here you are, my little croodlin doo!
Looked in er cradle, but did n't find you there,
Looked f r my wee, wee croodlin doo ever'where;
Ben kind lonesome all er day withouten you;
Where you ben, my little wee, wee croodlin doo?

Now you go balow, my little croodlin doo;
Now you go rockaby ever so far,—
Rockaby, rockaby, up to the star
That's winkin' an' blinkin' an' singin' to you
As you go balow, my wee, wee croodlin doo!

THE "HAPPY ISLES" OF HORACE.

OH, come with me to the Happy Isles
In the golden haze off yonder,
Where the song of the sun-kissed breeze beguiles,
And the ocean loves to wander.

Fragrant the vines that mantle those hills,
Proudly the fig rejoices;
Merrily dance the virgin rills,
Blending their myriad voices.

Our herds shall fear no evil there,
But peacefully feed and rest them;
Neither shall serpent or prowling bear
Ever come there to molest them.

Neither shall Eurus, wanton bold,
Nor feverish drouth distress us,
But he that compasseth heat and cold
Shall temper them both to bless us.

There no vandal foot has trod,
And the pirate hosts that wander
Shall never profane the sacred sod
Of those beautiful Isles out yonder.

Never a spell shall blight our vines,
Nor Sinus blaze above us,
But you and I shall drink our wines
And sing to the loved that love us.

So come with me where Fortune smiles
And the gods invite devotion,—
Oh, come with me to the Happy Isles
In the haze of that far-off ocean!

DUTCH LULLABY.

WYNKEN, Blynken, and Nod one night
Sailed off in a wooden shoe,—
Sailed on a river of misty light
Into a sea of dew.
"Where are you going, and what do you wish?"
The old moon asked the three.
"We have come to fish for the herring-fish
That live in this beautiful sea;
Nets of silver and gold have we,"
Said Wynken,
Blynken,
And Nod.

The old moon laughed and sung a song,
As they rocked in the wooden shoe;
And the wind that sped them all night long
Ruffled the waves of dew;
The little stars were the herring-fish
That lived in the beautiful sea.

"Now cast your nets wherever you wish,
But never afeard are we!"
So cried the stars to the fishermen three,
Wynken,
Blynken,
And Nod.

All night long their nets they threw
For the fish in the twinkling foam,

Then down from the sky came the wooden shoe,
Bringing the fishermen home;
'T was all so pretty a sail, it seemed
As if it could not be;
And some folk thought 't was a dream they 'd dreamed
Of sailing that beautiful sea;
But I shall name you the fishermen three:
Wynken,
Blynken,
And Nod.

Wynken and Blynken are two little eyes,
And Nod is a little head,
And the wooden shoe that sailed the skies
Is a wee one's trundle-bed;

So shut your eyes while Mother sings
Of wonderful sights that be,
And you shall see the beautiful things
As you rock on the misty sea
Where the old shoe rocked the fishermen three,—
Wynken,
Blynken,
And Nod.

HUGO'S "FLOWER TO BUTTERFLY."

SWEET, bide with me and let my love
Be an enduring tether;
Oh, wanton not from spot to spot,
But let us dwell together.

You 've come each morn to sip the sweets

With which you found me dripping,
Yet never knew it was not dew
But tears that you were sipping.

You gambol over honey meads
Where siren bees are humming;
But mine the fate to watch and wait
For my beloved's coming.

The sunshine that delights you now
Shall fade to darkness gloomy;
You should not fear if, biding here,
You nestled closer to me.

So rest you, love, and be my love,
That my enraptured blooming
May fill your sight with tender light,
Your wings with sweet perfuming.

Or, if you will not bide with me
Upon this quiet heather,
Oh, give me wing, thou beauteous thing,
That we may soar together.

A PROPER TREWE IDYLL OF CAMELOT.

WHENAS ye plaisaunt Aperille shoures have washed and purged awaye
Ye poysons and ye rheums of earth to make a merrie May,
Ye shraddy boscage of ye woods ben full of birds that syng
Right merrilie a madrigal unto ye waking spring,
Ye whiles that when ye face of earth ben washed and wiped ycleane
Her peeping posies blink and stare like they had ben her een;
Then, wit ye well, ye harte of man ben turned to thoughts of love,

And, tho' it ben a lyon erst, it now ben like a dove!
And many a goodly damosel in innocence beguiles
Her owne trewe love with sweet discourse and divers plaisaunt wiles.
In soche a time ye noblesse liege that ben Kyng Arthure hight

Let cry a joust and tournament for evereche errant knyght,
And, lo! from distant Joyous-garde and eche adjacent spot
A company of noblesse lords fared unto Camelot,
Wherein were mighty feastings and passing merrie cheere,
And eke a deale of dismal dole, as you shall quickly heare.

It so befell upon a daye when jousts ben had and while
Sir Launcelot did ramp around ye ring in gallaunt style,
There came an horseman shriking sore and rashing wildly home,—
A mediaeval horseman with ye usual flecks of foame;
And he did brast into ye ring, wherein his horse did drop,
Upon ye which ye rider did with like abruptness stop,
And with fatigue and fearfulness continued in a swound
Ye space of half an hour or more before a leech was founde.

"Now tell me straight," quod Launcelot, "what varlet knyght you be,
Ere that I chine you with my sworde and cleave your harte in three!"
Then rolled that knyght his bloudy een, and answered with a groane,—
"By worthy God that hath me made and shope ye sun and mone,
There fareth hence an evil thing whose like ben never seene,
And tho' he sayeth nony worde, he bodethe ill, I ween.
So take your parting, evereche one, and gird you for ye fraye,—
By all that's pure, ye Divell sure doth trend his path this way!"
Ye which he quoth and fell again into a deadly swound,
And on that spot, perchance (God wot), his bones mought yet be founde.

Then evereche knight girt on his sworde and shield and hied him straight
To meet ye straunger sarasen hard by ye city gate;

Full sorely moaned ye damosels and tore their beau-tyse haire
For that they feared an hippogriff wolde come to eate them there;
But as they moaned and swounded there too numerous to relate,
Kyng Arthure and Sir Launcelot stode at ye city gate,
And at eche side and round about stode many a noblesse knyght
With helm and speare and sworde and shield and mickle valor dight

Anon there came a straunger, but not a gyaunt grim,
Nor yet a draggon,—but a person gangling, long, and slim;
Yclad he was in guise that ill-beseemed those knygtly days,
And there ben nony etiquette in his uplandish ways;
His raiment was of dusty gray, and perched above his lugs
There ben the very latest style of blacke and shiny pluggs;
His nose ben like a vulture beake, his blie ben swart of hue,
And curly ben ye whiskers through ye which ye zephyrs blewe
Of all ye een that ben yseene in countries far or nigh,
None nonywhere colde hold compare unto that straunger's eye;
It was an eye of soche a kind as never ben on sleepe,
Nor did it gleam with kindly beame, nor did not use to weepe;
But soche an eye ye widdow hath,—an hongrey eye and wan,
That spyeth for an oder chaunce whereby she may catch on;
An eye that winketh of itself, and sayeth by that winke
Ye which a maiden sholde not knowe nor never even thinke;
Which winke ben more exceeding swift nor human thought ben thunk,
And leaveth doubting if so be that winke ben really wunke;
And soch an eye ye catte-fysshe hath when that he ben on dead
And boyled a goodly time and served with capers on his head;

A rayless eye, a bead-like eye, whose famisht aspect shows
It hungereth for ye verdant banks whereon ye wild time grows;
An eye that hawketh up and down for evereche kind of game,
And, when he doth espy ye which, he tumbleth to ye same.

Now when he kenned Sir Launcelot in armor clad, he quod,
"Another put-a-nickel-in-and-see-me-work, be god!"
But when that he was ware a man ben standing in that suit,
Ye straunger threw up both his hands, and asked him not to shoote.

Then spake Kyng Arthure: " If soe be you mind to do no ill,
Come, enter into Camelot, and eat and drink your fill;
But say me first what you are hight, and what mought be your quest.

Ye straunger quod, " I 'm five feet ten, and fare me from ye West!"
"Sir Fivefeetten," Kyng Arthure said, " I bid you welcome here;
So make you merrie as you list with plaisaunt wine and cheere;
This very night shall be a feast soche like ben never seene,
And you shall be ye honored guest of Arthure and his queene.
Now take him, good sir Maligraunce, and entertain him well
Until soche time as he becomes our guest, as I you tell."

That night Kyng Arthure's table round with mighty care ben spread,
Ye oder knyghts sate all about, and Arthure at ye heade:
Oh, 't was a goodly spectacle to ken that noblesse liege
Dispensing hospitality from his commanding siege!
Ye pheasant and ye meate of boare, ye haunch of velvet doe,
Ye canvass hamme he them did serve, and many good things moe.

Until at last Kyng Arthure cried: "Let bring my wassail cup,
And let ye sound of joy go round,—I 'm going to set 'em up!
I 've pipes of Malmsey, May-wine, sack, metheglon, mead, and sherry,
Canary, Malvoisie, and Port, swete Muscadelle and perry;
Rochelle, Osey, and Romenay, Tyre, Rhenish, posset too,
With kags and pails of foaming ales of brown October brew.
To wine and beer and other cheere I pray you now despatch ye,
And for ensample, wit ye well, sweet sirs, I 'm looking at ye!"

Unto which toast of their liege lord ye oders in ye party
Did lout them low in humble wise and bid ye same drink hearty.
So then ben merrisome discourse and passing plaisaunt cheere,
And Arthure's tales of hippogriffs ben mervaillous to heare;

But stranger far than any tale told of those knights of old
Ben those facetious narratives ye Western straunger told.
He told them of a country many leagues beyond ye sea
Where evereche forraine nuisance but ye Chinese man ben free,
And whiles he span his monstrous yarns, ye ladies of ye court
Did deem ye listening thereunto to be right plaisaunt sport;
And whiles they listened, often he did squeeze a lily hande,—
Ye which proceeding ne'er before ben done in Arthure's lande;
And often wank a sidelong wink with either roving eye,
Whereat ye ladies laughen so that they had like to die.
But of ye damosels that sat around Kyng Arthure's table
He liked not her that sometime ben ron over by ye cable,

Ye which full evil hap had harmed and marked her person so
That in a passing wittie jest he dubbeth her ye crow.
But all ye oders of ye girls did please him passing well
And they did own him for to be a proper seeming swell;
And in especial Guinevere esteemed him wondrous faire,
Which had made Arthure and his friend, Sir
Launcelot, to sware
But that they both ben so far gone with posset, wine, and beer,
They colde not see ye carrying-on, nor neither colde not heare;
For of eche liquor Arthure quafft, and so did all ye rest,
Save only and excepting that smooth straunger from the West.
When as these oders drank a toast, he let them have their fun
With divers godless mixings, but he stock to willow run,

Ye which (and all that reade these words sholde profit by ye warning)
Doth never make ye head to feel like it ben swelled next morning.
Now, wit ye well, it so befell that when the night grew dim,
Ye Kyng was carried from ye hall with a howling jag on him,
Whiles Launcelot and all ye rest that to his highness toadied
Withdrew them from ye banquet hall and sought their couches loaded.

Now, lithe and listen, lordings all, whiles I do call it shame
That, making cheer with wine and beer, men do abuse ye same;
Though eche be well enow alone, ye mixing of ye two
Ben soche a piece of foolishness as only ejiots do.
Ye wine is plaisaunt bibbing whenas ye gentles dine,
And beer will do if one hath not ye wherewithal for wine,
But in ye drinking of ye same ye wise are never floored

By taking what ye tipplers call too big a jag on board.
Right hejeous is it for to see soche dronkonness of wine
Whereby some men are use to make themselves to be like swine;
And sorely it repenteth them, for when they wake next day
Ye fearful paynes they suffer ben soche as none mought say,
And soche ye brenning in ye throat and brasting of ye head
And soche ye taste within ye mouth like one had been on dead,—
Soche be ye foul condicions that these unhappy men
Sware they will never drink no drop of nony drinke again.
Yet all so frail and vain a thing and weak withal is man
That he goeth on an oder tear whenever that he can.
And like ye evil quatern or ye hills that skirt ye skies,
Ye jag is reproductive and jags on jags arise.

Whenas Aurora from ye east in dewy splendor hied
King Arthure dreemed he saw a snaix and ben on fire inside,
And waking from this hejeous dreeme he sate him up in bed,—
"What, ho! an absynthe cocktail, knave! And make it strong!" he said;

Then, looking down beside him, lo! his lady was not there—
He called, he searched, but, Goddis wounds! He found her nonywhere;
And whiles he searched, Sir Maligraunce rashed in, wood wroth, and cried,
"Methinketh that ye straunger knyght hath snuck away my bride!
And whiles he spake a motley score of other knyghts brast in
And filled ye royall chamber with a mickle fear-full din,
For evereche one had lost his wiffe nor colde not spye ye same,
Nor colde not spye ye straunger knyght, Sir
Fivefeetten of name.

Oh, then and there was grevious lamentacion all arounde,
For nony dame nor damosel in Camelot ben found,—
Gone, like ye forest leaves that speed afore ye autumn wind.
Of all ye ladies of that court not one ben left behind
Save only that same damosel ye straunger called ye crow,
And she allowed with moche regret she ben too lame to go;
And when that she had wept full sore, to Arthure she confess'd
That Guernevere had left this word for Arthure and ye rest:
"Tell them," she quod, "we shall return to them whenas we 've made
This little deal we have with ye Chicago Bourde of Trade."

BÉRANGER'S "MA VOCATION."

MISERY is my lot,
Poverty and pain;
Ill was I begot,
Ill must I remain;
Yet the wretched days
One sweet comfort bring,
When God whispering says,
"Sing, O singer, sing!"

Chariots rumble by,

Splashing me with mud;
Insolence see I
Fawn to royal blood;
Solace have I then
From each galling sting
In that voice again,—
"Sing, O singer, sing!"

Cowardly at heart,
I am forced to play
A degraded part
For its paltry pay;
Freedom is a prize
For no starving thing;
Yet that small voice cries,
"Sing, O singer, sing!"

I was young, but now,
When I 'm old and gray,
Love—I know not how
Or why—hath sped away;
Still, in winter days
As in hours of spring,
Still a whisper says,
"Sing, O singer, sing!"

Ah, too well I know
Song's my only friend!
Patiently I'll go
Singing to the end;
Comrades, to your wine!
Let your glasses ring!
Lo, that voice divine

Whispers, "Sing, oh, sing!"

CHILD AND MOTHER.

O MOTHER-MY-LOVE, if you 11 give me your hand,
And go where I ask you to wander,
I will lead you away to a beautiful land,—
The Dreamland that's waiting out yonder.
We 'll walk in a sweet posie-garden out there,
Where moonlight and starlight are streaming,
And the flowers and the birds are filling the air
With the fragrance and music of dreaming.

There 'll be no little tired-out boy to undress,
No questions or cares to perplex you,
There 'll be no little bruises or bumps to caress,
Nor patching of stockings to vex you;
For I'll rock you away on a silver-dew stream
And sing you asleep when you 're weary,
And no one shall know of our beautiful dream
But you and your own little dearie.

And when I am tired I'll nestle my head
In the bosom that's soothed me so often,
And the wide-awake stars shall sing, in my stead,
A song which our dreaming shall soften.
So, Mother-my-Love, let me take your dear hand,
And away through the starlight we 'll wander,—
Away through the mist to the beautiful land,—
The Dreamland that's waiting out yonder.

THE CONVERSAZZHYONY.

WHAT conversazzhyonies wuz I really did not know,
For that, you must remember, wuz a powerful spell ago;
The camp wuz new 'nd noisy, 'nd only modrit sized,
So fashionable sossiety wuz hardly crystallized.
There had n't been no grand events to interest the men,
But a lynchin', or a inquest, or a jackpot now an then.
The wimmin-folks wuz mighty scarce, for wimmin', ez a rool,
Don't go to Colorado much, excep' for teachin' school,
An' bein' scarce an' chipper and pretty (like as not),
The bachelors perpose, 'nd air accepted on the spot

Now Sorry Tom wuz owner uv the Gosh-all-Hem-lock mine,
The wich allowed his better haff to dress all-fired fine;
For Sorry Tom wuz mighty proud uv her, an' she uv him,
Though she wuz short an' tacky, an' he wuz tall an' slim,
An' she wuz edjicated, an' Sorry Tom wuz not,
Yet, for her sake, he 'd whack up every cussid cent he 'd got!
Waal, jest by way uv celebratin' matrimonial joys,
She thought she 'd give a conversazzhyony to the boys,—
A peert an' likely lady, 'nd ez full uv 'cute idees
'Nd uv etiquettish notions ez a fyste is full uv fleas.

Three-fingered Hoover kind uv kicked, an' said they might be durned
So fur ez any conversazzhyony wuz concerned;
He 'd come to Red Hoss Mountain to tunnel for the ore,
An' not to go to parties,—quite another kind uv bore!

But, bein' he wuz candidate for marshal uv the camp,
I rayther had the upper holts in arguin' with the scamp;
Sez I, "Three-fingered Hoover, can't ye see it is yer game

To go for all the votes ye kin an' collar uv the same?
"The wich perceivin'," Hoover sez, "Waal, ef I must, I must;
So I'll frequent that conversazzhyony, ef I bust!"

Three-fingered Hoover wuz a trump! Ez fine a man wuz he
Ez ever caused an inquest or blossomed on a tree!—
A big, broad man, whose face bespoke a honest heart within,—
With a bunch uv yaller whiskers appertainin' to his chin,
'Nd a fierce mustache turnt up so fur that both his ears wuz hid,
Like the picture that you always see in the "Life uv Cap'n Kidd."

His hair wuz long an' wavy an' fine ez Southdown fleece,—
Oh, it shone an' smelt like Eden when he slicked it down with grease!
I'll bet there wuz n't anywhere a man, all round, ez fine
Ez wuz Three-fingered Hoover in the spring uv '69!

The conversazzhyony wuz a notable affair,
The bong tong deckolett 'nd en regaly bein' there;
The ranch where Sorry Tom hung out wuz fitted up immense,—
The Denver papers called it a "palashal residence."
There wuz mountain pines an' fern an' flowers a-hangin' on the walls,
An' cheers an' hoss-hair sofies wuz a-settin' in the halls;
An' there wuz heaps uv pictures uv folks that lived down East,
Sech ez poets an' perfessers, an' last, but not the least,
Wuz a chromo uv old Fremont,—we liked that best, you bet,
For there's lots uv us old miners that is votin' for him yet!

When Sorry Tom received the gang perlitely at the door,
He said that keerds would be allowed upon the second floor;
And then he asked us would we like a drop uv ody vee.
Connivin' at his meanin', we responded promptly, "Wee."
A conversazzhyony is a thing where people speak
The langwidge in the which they air partickulerly weak:

"I see," sez Sorry Tom, "you grasp what that 'ere lingo means."
"You bet yer boots," sez Hoover; " I 've lived at Noo Orleens,
An', though I aint no Frenchie, nor kin unto the same,
I kin parly voo, an' git there, too, like Eli, toot lee mame!"

As speakin' French wuz not my forte,—not even oovry poo,—
I stuck to keerds ez played by them ez did not parly voo,

An' bein' how that poker wuz my most perficient game,
I poneyed up for 20 blues an' set into the same.
Three-fingered Hoover stayed behind an' parlyvood so well
That all the kramy delly krame allowed he wuz the belle.
The other candidate for marshal did n't have a show;
For, while Three-fingered Hoover parlyed, ez they said, tray bow,
Bill Goslin did n't know enough uv French to git along,
'Nd I reckon that he had what folks might call a movy tong.

From Denver they had freighted up a real piannyfort
Uv the warty-leg and pearl-around-the-keys-an' kiwer sort,
An', later in the evenin', Perfesser Vere de Blaw
Performed on that pianny, with considerble eclaw,
Sech high-toned opry airs ez one is apt to hear, you know,
When he rounds up down to Denver at a Emmy Abbitt show;

An' Barber Jim (a talented but ornery galoot)
Discoursed a obligatter, conny mory, on the floot,
'Til we, ez sot upstairs indulgin' in a quiet game,
Conveyed to Barber Jim our wish to compromise the same.

The maynoo that wuz spread that night wuz mighty hard to beat,—
Though somewhat awkward to pernounce, it wuz not so to eat:
There wuz puddins, pies, an' sandwidges, an' forty kinds uv sass,
An' floatin' Irelands, custards, tarts, an' patty dee foy grass;

An' millions uv cove oysters wuz a-settin' round in pans,
'Nd other native fruits an' things that grow out West in cans.
But I wuz all kufflummuxed when Hoover said he'd choose
"Oon peety morso, see voo play, de la cette Charlotte Rooze;"
I'd knowed Three-fingered Hoover for fifteen years or more,
'Nd I'd never heern him speak so light uv wimmia folks before!

Bill Goslin heern him say it, 'nd uv course he spread the news
Uv how Three-fingered Hoover had insulted Charlotte Rooze
At the conversazzhyony down at Sorry Tom's that night,
An' when they asked me, I allowed that Bill for once wuz right;
Although it broke my heart to see my friend go up the fluke,
We all opined his treatment uv the girl deserved rebuke.
It warnt no use for Sorry Tom to nail it for a lie,–
When it come to sassin' wimmin, there wuz blood in every eye;
The boom for Charlotte Rooze swep' on an' took the polls by storm,
An' so Three-fingered Hoover fell a martyr to reform!

Three-fingered Hoover said it wuz a terrible mistake,
An' when the votes wuz in, he cried ez if his heart would break.

We never knew who Charlotte wuz, but Goslin's brother Dick
Allowed she wuz the teacher from the camp on Roarin' Crick,
That had come to pass some foreign tongue with them uv our alite
Ez wuz at the high-toned party down at Sorry Tom's that night.
We let it drop—this matter uv the lady—there an' then,
An' we never heerd, nor wanted to, of Charlotte Rooze again,
An' the Colorado wimmin-folks, ez like ez not, don't know
How we vindicated all their sex a twenty year ago.

For in these wondrous twenty years has come a mighty change,
An' most uv them old pioneers have gone acrosst the range,
Way out into the silver land beyond the peaks uv snow,—

The land uv rest an' sunshine, where all good miners go.

I reckon that they love to look, from out the silver haze,
Upon that God's own country where they spent sech happy days;
Upon the noble cities that have risen since they went;
Upon the camps an' ranches that are prosperous an' content;
An', best uv all, upon those hills that reach into the air,
Ez if to clasp the loved ones that are waitin' over there.

PROF. VERE DE BLAW.

ACHIEVIN' sech distinction with his model tabble dote
Ez to make his Red Hoss Mountain restauraw a place uv note,
Our old friend Casey innovated somewhat round the place,
In hopes he would ameliorate the sufferins uv the race;
'Nd uv the many features Casey managed to import
The most important wuz a Steenway gran' piannyfort,
An' bein' there wuz nobody could play upon the same,
He telegraffed to Denver, 'nd a real perfesser came,—

The last an' crownin' glory uv the Casey restauraw
Wuz that tenderfoot musicianer, Perfesser Vere de Blaw!

His hair wuz long an' dishybyi, an' he had a yaller skin,
An' the absence uv a collar made his neck look powerful thin:
A sorry man he wuz to see, az mebby you 'd surmise,
But the fire uv inspiration wuz a-blazin' in his eyes!
His name wuz Blanc, wich same is Blaw (for that's what Casey said,
An' Casey passed the French ez well ez any Frenchie bred);
But no one ever reckoned that it really wuz his name,
An' no one ever asked him how or why or whence he came,—
Your ancient history is a thing the Coloradan hates,
An' no one asks another what his name wuz in the States!

At evenin', when the work wuz done, an' the miners rounded up
At Casey's, to indulge in keerds or linger with the cup,
Or dally with the tabble dote in all its native glory,
Perfesser Vere de Blaw discoursed his music repertory
Upon the Steenway gran' piannyfort, the wich wuz sot
In the hallway near the kitchen (a warm but quiet spot),
An' when De Blaw's environments induced the proper pride,—
Wich gen'rally wuz whiskey straight, with seltzer on the side,—
He throwed his soulful bein' into opry airs 'nd things
Wich bounded to the ceilin' like he 'd mesmerized the strings.

Oh, you that live in cities where the gran' piannies grow,
An' primy donnies round up, it's little that you know

Uv the hungerin' an' the yearnin' wich us miners an' the rest
Feel for the songs we used to hear before we moved out West.
Yes, memory is a pleasant thing, but it weakens mighty quick;
It kind uv dries an' withers, like the windin' mountain crick,
That, beautiful, an' singin' songs, goes dancin' to the plains,
So long ez it is fed by snows an' watered by the rains;
But, uv that grace uv luvin' rains 'nd mountain snows bereft,
Its bleachin' rocks, like dummy ghosts, is all its memory left

The toons wich the perfesser would perform with sech eclaw
Would melt the toughest mountain gentleman I ever saw,—
Sech touchin' opry music ez the Trovytory sort,
The solium "Mizer Reery," an' the thrillin' "Keely Mort;"

Or, sometimes, from "Lee Grond Dooshess" a trifle he would play,
Or morsoze from a opry boof, to drive dull care away;
Or, feelin' kind uv serious, he'd discourse somewhat in C,—
The wich he called a opus (whatever that may be);

But the toons that fetched the likker from the critics in the crowd
Wuz not the high-toned ones, Perfesser Vere de Blaw allowed.

'Twuz "Dearest May," an' "Bonnie Doon," an' the ballard uv "Ben Bolt,"
Ez wuz regarded by all odds ez Vere de Blaw's best holt;
Then there wuz "Darlin' Nellie Gray," an'"Settin' on the Stile,"
An' "Seein' Nellie Home," an' "Nancy Lee," 'nd
"Annie Lisle,"
An' "Silver Threads among the Gold," an' "The Gal that Winked at Me,"
An' "Gentie Annie," "Nancy Till," an' "The Cot beside the Sea."

Your opry airs is good enough for them ez likes to pay
Their money for the truck ez can't be got no other way;
But opry to a miner is a thin an' holler thing,—
The music that he pines for is the songs he used to sing.

One evenin' down at Casey's De Blaw wuz at his best,
With four-fingers uv old Wilier-run concealed beneath his vest;
The boys wuz settin' all around, discussin' folks an' things,
'Nd I had drawed the necessary keerds to fill on kings;
Three-fingered Hoover kind uv leaned acrosst the bar to say
If Casey 'd liquidate right off, he 'd liquidate next day;
A sperrit uv contentment wuz a-broodin' all around
(Onlike the other sperrits wich in restauraws abound),
When, suddenly, we heerd from yonder kitchen-entry rise

A toon each ornery galoot appeared to recognize.
Perfesser Vere de Blaw for once eschewed his opry ways,
An' the remnants uv his mind went back to earlier, happier days,
An' grappled like an' wrassled with a old familiar air
The wich we all uv us had heern, ez you have, everywhere!
Stock still we stopped,—some in their talk uv politics an' things,
I in my unobtrusive attempt to fill on kings,

'Nd Hoover leanin' on the bar, an' Casey at the till,—
We all stopped short an' held our breaths (ez a feller sometimes will),
An' sot there more like bumps on logs than healthy, husky men,
Ez the memories uv that old, old toon come sneakin' back again.

You've guessed it? No, you have n't; for it wuz n't that there song
Uv the home we 'd been away from an' had hankered for so long,—

No, sir; it wuz n't u Home, Sweet Home," though
it's always heard around
Sech neighborhoods in wich the home that is "sweet home" is found.
And, ez for me, I seemed to see the past come back again,
And hear the deep-drawed sigh my sister Lucy uttered when
Her mother asked her if she 'd practised her two hours that day,
Wich, if she had n't, she must go an' do it right away!
The homestead in the States 'nd all its memories seemed to come
A-floatin' round about me with that magic lumtytum.

And then uprose a stranger wich had struck the camp that night;
His eyes wuz sot an' fireless, 'nd his face wuz spookish white,
'Nd he sez: " Oh, how I suffer there is nobody kin say,
Onless, like me, he's wrenched himself from home an' friends away

To seek surcease from sorrer in a fur, seclooded spot,
Only to find—alars, too late!—the wich surcease is not!
Only to find that there air things that, somehow, seem to live
For nothin' in the world but jest the misery they give!
I 've travelled eighteen hundred miles, but that toon has got here first;
I 'm done,—I 'm blowed,—I welcome death, an' bid it do its worst!"

Then, like a man whose mind wuz sot on yieldin' to his fate,
He waltzed up to the counter an' demanded whiskey straight,
Wich havin' got outside uv,—both the likker and the door,—

We never seen that stranger in the bloom uv health no more!
But some months later, what the birds had left uv him wuz found
Associated with a tree, some distance from the ground;

And Husky Sam, the coroner, that set upon him, said
That two things wuz apparent, namely: first, deceast wuz dead;
And, second, previously had got involved beyond all hope
In a knotty complication with a yard or two uv rope!

MEDIAEVAL EVENTIDE SONG.

COME hither, lyttel childe, and lie upon my breast to-night,
For yonder fares an angell yclad in raimaunt white,
And yonder sings ye angell as onely angells may,
And his songe ben of a garden that bloometh farre awaye.

To them that have no lyttel childe Godde sometimes sendeth down
A lyttel childe that ben a lyttel lambkyn of his owne;
And if so bee they love that childe, He willeth it to staye,
But elsewise, in His mercie He taketh it awaye.

And sometimes, though they love it, Godde yearn-eth for ye childe,
And sendeth angells singing, whereby it ben beguiled;
They fold their arms about ye lamb that croodleth at bis play,
And beare him to ye garden that bloometh farre awaye.

I wolde not lose ye.lyttel lamb that Godde hath lent to me;
If I colde sing that angell songe, how joysome I sholde bee!
For, with mine arms about him, and my musick in his eare,
What angell songe of paradize soever sholde I feare?

Soe come, my lyttel childe, and lie upon my breast to-night,
For yonder fares an angell yclad in raimaunt white,

And yonder sings that angell, as onely angells may,
And his songe ben of a garden that bloometh farre awaye.

MARTHY'S YOUNKIT.

THE mountain brook sung lonesomelike, and loitered on its way
Ez if it waited for a child to jine it in its play;
The wild-flowers uv the hillside bent down their heads to hear
The music uv the little feet that had somehow grown so dear;
The magpies, like winged shadders, wuz a-flutterin' to an' fro
Among the rocks an' holler stumps in the ragged gulch below;
The pines an' hemlocks tosst their boughs (like they wuz arms) and made
Soft, solium music on the slope where he had often played;
But for these lonesome, solium voices on the mountain-side,
There wuz no sound the summer day that Marthy's younkit died.

We called him Marthy's younkit, for Marthy wuz the name
Uv her ez wuz his mar, the wife uv Sorry Tom,—the same
Ez taught the school-house on the hill, way back in '69,
When she marr'd Sorry Tom, wich owned the Gosh-all-Hemlock mine!
And Marthy's younkit wuz their first, wich, bein' how it meant
The first on Red Hoss Mountain, wuz truly a event!
The miners sawed off short on work ez soon ez
they got word
That Dock Devine allowed to Casey what had just occurred;
We loaded up an' whooped around until we all wuz hoarse
Salutin' the arrival, wich weighed ten pounds, uv course!

Three years, and sech a pretty child!—his mother's counterpart!
Three years, and sech a holt ez he had got on every heart!—

A peert an' likely little tyke with hair ez red ez gold,
A laughin', toddlin' everywhere,—'nd only three years old!

Up yonder, sometimes, to the store, an' sometimes down the hill
He kited (boys is boys, you know,—you couldn't keep him still!)
An' there he 'd play beside the brook where purpul wild-flowers grew,
An' the mountain pines an' hemlocks a kindly shadder threw,
An' sung soft, solium toons to him, while in the gulch below
The magpies, like strange sperrits, went flutterin' to an' fro.

Three years, an' then the fever come,—it wuz n't right, you know,
With all us old ones in the camp, for that little child to go;
It's right the old should die, but that a harmless little child
Should miss the joy uv life an' love,—that can't be reconciled!

That's what we thought that summer day, an' that is what we said
Ez we looked upon the piteous face uv Marthy's younkit dead.
But for his mother's sobbin', the house wuz very still,
An' Sorry Tom wuz lookin', through the winder, down the hill,
To the patch beneath the hemlocks where his darlin' used to play,
An' the mountain brook sung lonesomelike an' loitered on its way.

A preacher come from Roarin' Crick to comfort 'em an' pray,
'Nd all the camp wuz present at the obsequies next day;
A female teacher staged it twenty miles to sing a hymn,
An' we jined her in the chorus,—big, husky men an' grim
Sung "Jesus, Lover uv my Soul," an' then the preacher prayed,
An' preacht a sermon on the death uv that fair blossom laid

Among them other flowers he loved,—wich sermon set sech weight
On sinners bein' always heeled against the future state,
That, though it had been fashionable to swear a perfec' streak,
There warnt no swearin' in the camp for pretty nigh a week!

Last thing uv all, four strappin' men took up the little load
An' bore it tenderly along the winding rocky road,

To where the coroner had dug a grave beside the brook,
In sight uv Marthy's winder, where the same could set an' look
An' wonder if his cradle in that green patch, long an' wide,
Wuz ez sooth in' ez the cradle that wuz empty at her side;
An' wonder if the mournful songs the pines wuz singin' then
Wuz ez tender ez the lullabies she'd never sing again,
'Nd if the bosom uv the earth in wich he lay at rest
Wuz half ez lovin' 'nd ez warm ez wuz his mother's breast

The camp is gone; but Red Hoss Mountain rears its kindly head,
An' looks down, sort uv tenderly, upon its cherished dead;
'Nd I reckon that, through all the years, that little boy wich died
Sleeps sweetly an' contentedly upon the mountainside;
That the wild-flowers uv the summer-time bend down their heads to hear
The footfall uv a little friend they know not slumbers near;
That the magpies on the solium rocks strange . flutterin' shadders make,
An' the pines an' hemlocks wonder that the sleeper does n't wake;
That the mountain brook sings lonesomelike an' loiters on its way
Ez if it waited for a child to jine it in its play.

IN FLANDERS.

THROUGH sleet and fogs to the saline bogs
Where the herring fish meanders,
An army sped, and then, 't is said,
Swore terribly in Flanders:
    " _____ _____ _____ _____!"
    " _____ _____ _____ _____!"

A hideous store of oaths they swore,
Did the army over in Flanders!

At this distant day we 're unable to say

What so aroused their danders;
But it's doubtless the case, to their lasting disgrace,
That the army swore in Flanders:
"_____ _____ _____ _____!"
"_____ _____ _____ _____!"

And many more such oaths they swore,
Did that impious horde in Flanders!

Some folks contend that these oaths without end
Began among the commanders,
That, taking this cue, the subordinates, too,
Swore terribly in Flanders:
'T was "_____ _____ _____!"
"_____ _____ _____!"

Why, the air was blue with the hullabaloo
Of those wicked men in Flanders!

But some suppose that the trouble arose
With a certain Corporal Sanders,
Who sought to abuse the wooden shoes
That the natives wore in Flanders.
Saying: "_____ _____ _____!"
"_____ _____ _____!"

What marvel then, that the other men
Felt encouraged to swear in Flanders!

At any rate, as I grieve to state,
Since these soldiers vented their danders
Conjectures obtain that for language profane
There is no such place as Flanders.

"_____ _____ _____ _____!"
"_____ _____ _____ _____!"
This is the kind of talk you 'll find
If ever you go to Flanders.

How wretched is he, wherever he be,
That unto this habit panders!
And how glad am I that my interests lie
In Chicago, and not in Flanders!
"_____ _____ _____ _____!"
"_____ _____ _____ _____!"
Would never go down in this circumspect town
However it might in Flanders.

OUR BIGGEST FISH.

WHEN in the halcyon days of eld, I was a little tyke,
I used to fish In pickerel ponds for minnows and the like;
And oh, the bitter sadness with which my soul was fraught
When I rambled home at nightfall with the puny string I 'd caught!
And, oh, the indignation and the valor I 'd display
When I claimed that all the biggest fish I 'd caught had got away!

Sometimes it was the rusty hooks, sometimes the fragile lines,
And many times the treacherous reeds would foil my just designs;
But whether hooks or lines or reeds were actually to blame
I kept right on at losing all the monsters just the same—
I never lost a little fish—yes, I am free to say
It always was the biggest fish I caught that got away.

And so it was, when later on, I felt ambition pass
From callow minnow joys to nobler greed for pike and bass;

I found it quite convenient, when the beauties would n't bite
And I returned all bootless from the watery chase at night,
To feign a cheery aspect and recount in accents gay
How the biggest fish that I had taught had somehow got away.

And really, fish look bigger than they are before they're caught—
When the pole is bent into a bow and the slender line is taut,
When a fellow feels his heart rise up like a doughnut in his throat
And he lunges in a frenzy up and down the leaky boat!
Oh, you who've been a-fishing will indorse me when I say
That it always is the biggest fish you catch that gets away!

'T is even so in other things—yes, in our greedy eyes
The biggest boon is some elusive, never-captured prize;
We angle for the honors and the sweets of human life—
Like fishermen we brave the seas that roll in endless strife;
And then at last, when all is done and we are spent and gray,
We own the biggest fish we've caught are those that got away.

I would not have it otherwise; 'tis better there should be
Much bigger fish than I have caught a-swimming in the sea;
For now some worthier one than I may angle for that game—

May by his arts entice, entrap, and comprehend the same;
Which, having done, perchance he 'll bless the man who's proud to say
That the biggest fish he ever caught were those that got away.

THIRTY-NINE.

O HAPLESS day! O wretched day!
I hoped you 'd pass me by—
Alas, the years have sneaked away
And all is changed but I!

Had I the power, I would remand
You to a gloom condign,
But here you 've crept upon me and
I—I am thirty-nine I

Now, were I thirty-five, I could
Assume a flippant guise;
Or, were I forty years, I should
Undoubtedly look wise;
For forty years are said to bring
Sedateness superfine;
But thirty-nine donft mean a thing—
A bos with thirty-nine!

You healthy, hulking girls and boys,—
What makes you grow so fast?
Oh, I'll survive your lusty noise—
I 'm tough and bound to last!
No, no—I 'm old and withered too—
I feel my powers decline,
(Yet none believes this can be true
Of one at thirty-nine).

And you, dear girl with velvet eyes,
I wonder what you mean
Through all our keen anxieties
By keeping sweet sixteen.
With your dear love to warm my heart,
Wretch were I to repine;
I was but jesting at the start—
I 'm glad I 'm thirty-nine!

So, little children, roar and race

As blithely as you can,
And, sweetheart, let your tender grace
Exalt the Day and Man;
For then these factors (I'll engage)
All subtly shall combine
To make both juvenile and sage
The one who's thirty-nine!

Yes, after all, I 'm free to say
I would much rather be
Standing as I do stand to-day,
Twixt devil and deep sea;
For though my face be dark with care
Or with a grimace shine,
Each haply falls unto my share,
For I am thirty-nine!

'T is passing meet to make good cheer
And lord it like a king,
Since only once we catch the year
That does n't mean a thing.
O happy day! O gracious day!
I pledge thee in this wine—
Come, let us journey on our way
A year, good Thirty-Nine!

Sept. 2,1889.

YVYTOT.

WHERE wail the waters in their flow
A spectre wanders to and fro,
And evermore that ghostly shore

Bemoans the heir of Yvytot.

Sometimes 1 when, like a fleecy pall,
The mists upon the waters fall,
Across the main float shadows twain
That do not heed the spectre's call.

The king his son of Yvytot
Stood once and saw the waters go
Boiling around with hissing sound
The sullen phantom rocks below.

And suddenly he saw a face
Lift from that black and seething place—
Lift up and gaze in mute amaze
And tenderly a little space,

A mighty cry of love made he—
No answering word to him gave she,
But looked, and then sunk back again
Into the dark and depthless sea.

And ever afterward that face,
That he beheld such little space,
Like wraith would rise within his eyes
And in his heart find biding place.

So oft from castle hall he crept
Where mid the rocks grim shadows slept,
And where the mist reached down and kissed
The waters as they wailed and wept.

The king it was of Yvytot

That vaunted, many years ago,
There was no coast his valiant host
Had not subdued with spear and bow.

For once to him the sea-king cried:
"In safety all thy ships shall ride
An thou but swear thy princely heir
Shall take my daughter to his bride.

"And lo, these winds that rove the sea
Unto our pact shall witness be,
And of the oath which binds us both
Shall be the judge 'twixt me and thee!"

Then swore the king of Yvytot
Unto the sea-king years ago,
And with great cheer for many a year
His ships went harrying to and fro.

Unto this mighty king his throne
Was born a prince, and one alone—
Fairer than he in form and blee
And knightly grace was never known.

But once he saw a maiden face
Lift from a haunted ocean place—
Lift up and gaze in mute amaze
And tenderly a little space.

Wroth was the king of Yvytot,
For that his son would never go
Sailing the sea, but liefer be
Where wailed the waters in their flow,

Where winds in clamorous anger swept,
Where to and fro grim shadows crept,
And where the mist reached down and kissed
The waters as they wailed and wept

So sped the years, till came a day
The haughty king was old and gray,
And in his hold were spoils untold
That he had wrenched from Norroway.

Then once again the sea-king cried:
"Thy ships have harried far and wide;
My part is done—now let thy son
Require my daughter to his bride!"

Loud laughed the king of Yvytot,
And by his soul he bade him no—
"I heed no more what oath I swore,
For I was mad to bargain so!"

Then spake the sea-king in his wrath:
"Thy ships lie broken in my path!
Go now and wring thy hands, false king!
Nor ship nor heir thy kingdom hath!

"And thou shalt wander evermore
All up and down this ghostly shore,
And call in vain upon the twain
That keep what oath a dastard swore!"

The king his son of Yvytot
Stood even then where to and fro
The breakers swelled—and there beheld

A maiden face lift from below

"Be thou or truth or dream," he cried,
"Or spirit of the restless tide,
It booteth not to me, God wot!
But I would have thee to my bride."

Then spake the maiden: "Come with me
Unto a palace in the sea,
For there my sire in kingly ire
Requires thy king his oath of thee!"

Gayly he fared him down the sands
And took the maiden's outstretched hands;
And so went they upon their way
To do the sea-king his commands.

And lo! to-night, the phantom light,
That, as a sprite, flits on the fender,
Reveals a face whose girlish grace
Brings back the feeling, warm and tender;
And, all the while, the old-time smile
Plays on my visage, grim and wrinkled,—
As though, soubrette, your footfalls yet
Upon my rusty heart-strings tinkled!

SOME TIME.

LAST night, my darling, as you slept,
I thought I heard you sigh,
And to your little crib I crept,
And watched a space thereby;
And then I stooped and kissed your brow,

For oh! I love you so—
You are too young to know it now,
But some time you shall know!

Some time when, in a darkened place
Where others come to weep,
Your eyes shall look upon a face
Calm in eternal sleep,
The voiceless lips, the wrinkled brow,
The patient smile shall show—
You are too young to know it now,
But some time you may know!

Look backward; then, into the years,
And see me here to-night—
See, O my darling! how my tears
Are falling as I write;
And feel once more upon your brow
The kiss of long ago—
You are too young to know it now,
But some time you shall know.

THE END.

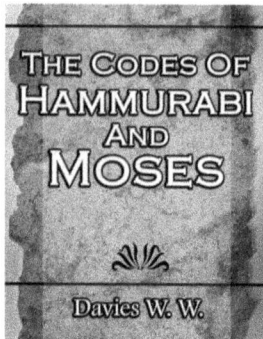

The Codes Of Hammurabi And Moses
W. W. Davies

QTY

The discovery of the Hammurabi Code is one of the greatest achievements of archaeology, and is of para-mount interest, not only to the student of the Bible, but also to all those interested in ancient history...

Religion   **ISBN:** *1-59462-338-4*   **Pages:132**
MSRP $12.95

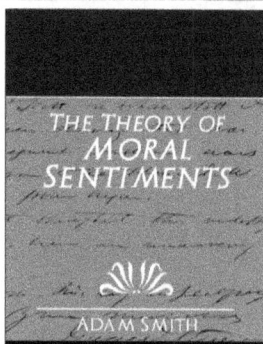

The Theory of Moral Sentiments
Adam Smith

QTY

This work from 1749. contains original theories of con-science amd moral judgment and it is the foundation for systemof morals.

Philosophy   **ISBN:** *1-59462-777-0*   **Pages:536**
MSRP $19.95

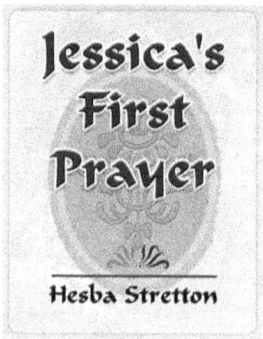

Jessica's First Prayer
Hesba Stretton

QTY

In a screened and secluded corner of one of the many railway-bridges which span the streets of London there could be seen a few years ago, from five o'clock every morning until half past eight, a tidily set-out coffee-stall, consisting of a trestle and board, upon which stood two large tin cans, with a small fire of charcoal burning under each so as to keep the coffee boiling during the early hours of the morning when the work-people were thronging into the city on their way to their daily toil...

Pages:84

Childrens   **ISBN:** *1-59462-373-2*   *MSRP $9.95*

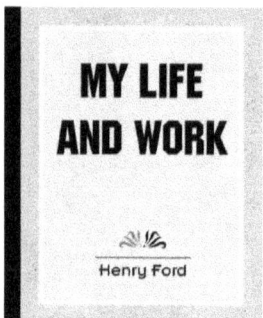

My Life and Work
Henry Ford

QTY

Henry Ford revolutionized the world with his implementation of mass production for the Model T automobile. Gain valuable business insight into his life and work with his own auto-biography... "We have only started on our development of our country we have not as yet, with all our talk of wonderful progress, done more than scratch the surface. The progress has been wonderful enough but..."

Pages:300

Biographies/   **ISBN:** *1-59462-198-5*   *MSRP $21.95*

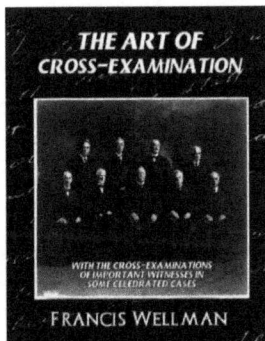

The Art of Cross-Examination
Francis Wellman

QTY

I presume it is the experience of every author, after his first book is published upon an important subject, to be almost overwhelmed with a wealth of ideas and illustrations which could readily have been included in his book, and which to his own mind, at least, seem to make a second edition inevitable. Such certainly was the case with me; and when the first edition had reached its sixth impression in five months, I rejoiced to learn that it seemed to my publishers that the book had met with a sufficiently favorable reception to justify a second and considerably enlarged edition. ...

Reference ISBN: *1-59462-647-2*

Pages:412

MSRP $19.95

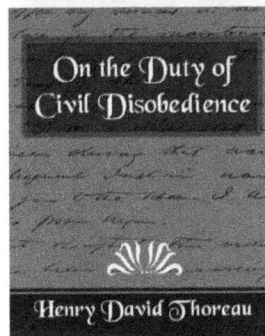

On the Duty of Civil Disobedience
Henry David Thoreau

QTY

Thoreau wrote his famous essay, On the Duty of Civil Disobedience, as a protest against an unjust but popular war and the immoral but popular institution of slave-owning. He did more than write—he declined to pay his taxes, and was hauled off to gaol in consequence. Who can say how much this refusal of his hastened the end of the war and of slavery ?

Law ISBN: *1-59462-747-9*

Pages:48

MSRP $7.45

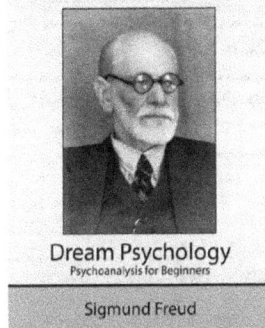

Dream Psychology Psychoanalysis for Beginners
Sigmund Freud

QTY

Sigmund Freud, born Sigismund Schlomo Freud (May 6, 1856 - September 23, 1939), was a Jewish-Austrian neurologist and psychiatrist who co-founded the psychoanalytic school of psychology. Freud is best known for his theories of the unconscious mind, especially involving the mechanism of repression; his redefinition of sexual desire as mobile and directed towards a wide variety of objects; and his therapeutic techniques, especially his understanding of transference in the therapeutic relationship and the presumed value of dreams as sources of insight into unconscious desires.

Psychology ISBN: *1-59462-905-6*

Pages:196

MSRP $15.45

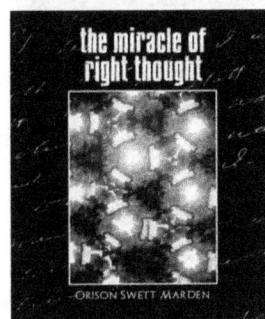

The Miracle of Right Thought
Orison Swett Marden

QTY

Believe with all of your heart that you will do what you were made to do. When the mind has once formed the habit of holding cheerful, happy, prosperous pictures, it will not be easy to form the opposite habit. It does not matter how improbable or how far away this realization may see, or how dark the prospects may be, if we visualize them as best we can, as vividly as possible, hold tenaciously to them and vigorously struggle to attain them, they will gradually become actualized, realized in the life. But a desire, a longing without endeavor, a yearning abandoned or held indifferently will vanish without realization.

Pages:360

Self Help ISBN: *1-59462-644-8*

MSRP $25.45

QTY

The Rosicrucian Cosmo-Conception Mystic Christianity by *Max Heindel*   ISBN: *1-59462-188-8*   **$38.95**
The Rosicrucian Cosmo-conception is not dogmatic, neither does it appeal to any other authority than the reason of the student. It is: not controversial, but is: sent forth in the, hope that it may help to clear...   New Age/Religion Pages 646

Abandonment To Divine Providence by *Jean-Pierre de Caussade*   ISBN: *1-59462-228-0*   **$25.95**
"The Rev. Jean Pierre de Caussade was one of the most remarkable spiritual writers of the Society of Jesus in France in the 18th Century. His death took place at Toulouse in 1751. His works have gone through many editions and have been republished...   Inspirational/Religion Pages 400

Mental Chemistry by *Charles Haanel*   ISBN: *1-59462-192-6*   **$23.95**
Mental Chemistry allows the change of material conditions by combining and appropriately utilizing the power of the mind. Much like applied chemistry creates something new and unique out of careful combinations of chemicals the mastery of mental chemistry...   New Age Pages 354

The Letters of Robert Browning and Elizabeth Barret Barrett 1845-1846 vol II   ISBN: *1-59462-193-4*   **$35.95**
by *Robert Browning* and *Elizabeth Barrett*   Biographies Pages 596

Gleanings In Genesis (volume I) by *Arthur W. Pink*   ISBN: *1-59462-130-6*   **$27.45**
Appropriately has Genesis been termed "the seed plot of the Bible" for in it we have, in germ form, almost all of the great doctrines which are afterwards fully developed in the books of Scripture which follow...   Religion/Inspirational Pages 420

The Master Key by *L. W. de Laurence*   ISBN: *1-59462-001-6*   **$30.95**
In no branch of human knowledge has there been a more lively increase of the spirit of research during the past few years than in the study of Psychology, Concentration and Mental Discipline. The requests for authentic lessons in Thought Control, Mental Discipline and...   New Age/Business Pages 422

The Lesser Key Of Solomon Goetia by *L. W. de Laurence*   ISBN: *1-59462-092-X*   **$9.95**
This translation of the first book of the "Lernegton" which is now for the first time made accessible to students of Talismanic Magic was done, after careful collation and edition, from numerous Ancient Manuscripts in Hebrew, Latin, and French...   New Age/Occult Pages 92

Rubaiyat Of Omar Khayyam by *Edward Fitzgerald*   ISBN:*1-59462-332-5*   **$13.95**
Edward Fitzgerald, whom the world has already learned, in spite of his own efforts to remain within the shadow of anonymity, to look upon as one of the rarest poets of the century, was born at Bredfield, in Suffolk, on the 31st of March, 1809. He was the third son of John Purcell...   Music Pages 172

Ancient Law by *Henry Maine*   ISBN: *1-59462-128-4*   **$29.95**
The chief object of the following pages is to indicate some of the earliest ideas of mankind, as they are reflected in Ancient Law, and to point out the relation of those ideas to modern thought.   Religiom/History Pages 452

Far-Away Stories by *William J. Locke*   ISBN: *1-59462-129-2*   **$19.45**
"Good wine needs no bush, but a collection of mixed vintages does. And this book is just such a collection. Some of the stories I do not want to remain buried for ever in the museum files of dead magazine-numbers an author's not unpardonable vanity..."   Fiction Pages 272

Life of David Crockett by *David Crockett*   ISBN: *1-59462-250-7*   **$27.45**
"Colonel David Crockett was one of the most remarkable men of the times in which he lived. Born in humble life, but gifted with a strong will, an indomitable courage, and unremitting perseverance...   Biographies/New Age Pages 424

Lip-Reading by *Edward Nitchie*   ISBN: *1-59462-206-X*   **$25.95**
Edward B. Nitchie, founder of the New York School for the Hard of Hearing, now the Nitchie School of Lip-Reading, Inc, wrote "LIP-READING Principles and Practice". The development and perfecting of this meritorious work on lip-reading was an undertaking...   How-to Pages 400

A Handbook of Suggestive Therapeutics, Applied Hypnotism, Psychic Science   ISBN: *1-59462-214-0*   **$24.95**
by *Henry Munro*   Health/New Age/Health/Self-help Pages 376

A Doll's House: and Two Other Plays by *Henrik Ibsen*   ISBN: *1-59462-112-8*   **$19.95**
Henrik Ibsen created this classic when in revolutionary 1848 Rome. Introducing some striking concepts in playwriting for the realist genre, this play has been studied the world over.   Fiction/Classics/Plays 308

The Light of Asia by *sir Edwin Arnold*   ISBN: *1-59462-204-3*   **$13.95**
In this poetic masterpiece, Edwin Arnold describes the life and teachings of Buddha. The man who was to become known as Buddha to the world was born as Prince Gautama of India but he rejected the worldly riches and abandoned the reigns of power when...   Religion/History/Biographies Pages 170

The Complete Works of Guy de Maupassant by *Guy de Maupassant*   ISBN: *1-59462-157-8*   **$16.95**
"For days and days, nights and nights, I had dreamed of that first kiss which was to consecrate our engagement, and I knew not on what spot I should put my lips..."   Fiction/Classics Pages 240

The Art of Cross-Examination by *Francis L. Wellman*   ISBN: *1-59462-309-0*   **$26.95**
Written by a renowned trial lawyer, Wellman imparts his experience and uses case studies to explain how to use psychology to extract desired information through questioning.   How-to/Science/Reference Pages 408

Answered or Unanswered? by *Louisa Vaughan*   ISBN: *1-59462-248-5*   **$10.95**
Miracles of Faith in China   Religion Pages 112

The Edinburgh Lectures on Mental Science (1909) by *Thomas*   ISBN: *1-59462-008-3*   **$11.95**
This book contains the substance of a course of lectures recently given by the writer in the Queen Street Hail, Edinburgh. Its purpose is to indicate the Natural Principles governing the relation between Mental Action and Material Conditions...   New Age/Psychology Pages 148

Ayesha by *H. Rider Haggard*   ISBN: *1-59462-301-5*   **$24.95**
Verily and indeed it is the unexpected that happens! Probably if there was one person upon the earth from whom the Editor of this, and of a certain previous history, did not expect to hear again...   Classics Pages 380

Ayala's Angel by *Anthony Trollope*   ISBN: *1-59462-352-X*   **$29.95**
The two girls were both pretty, but Lucy who was twenty-one who supposed to be simple and comparatively unattractive, whereas Ayala was credited, as her Bombwhat romantic name might show, with poetic charm and a taste for romance. Ayala when her father died was nineteen...   Fiction Pages 484

The American Commonwealth by *James Bryce*   ISBN: *1-59462-286-8*   **$34.45**
An interpretation of American democratic political theory. It examines political mechanics and society from the perspective of Scotsman James Bryce   Politics Pages 572

Stories of the Pilgrims by *Margaret P. Pumphrey*   ISBN: *1-59462-116-0*   **$17.95**
This book explores pilgrims religious oppression in England as well as their escape to Holland and eventual crossing to America on the Mayflower, and their early days in New England...   History Pages 268

QTY

The Fasting Cure by *Sinclair Upton*   ISBN: *1-59462-222-1* **$13.95** ☐
In the Cosmopolitan Magazine for May, 1910, and in the Contemporary Review (London) for April, 1910, I published an article dealing with my experiences in fasting. I have written a great many magazine articles, but never one which attracted so much attention... New Age/Self Help/Health Pages 164

Hebrew Astrology by *Sepharial*   ISBN: *1-59462-308-2* **$13.45** ☐
In these days of advanced thinking it is a matter of common observation that we have left many of the old landmarks behind and that we are now pressing forward to greater heights and to a wider horizon than that which represented the mind-content of our progenitors... Astrology Pages 144

Thought Vibration or The Law of Attraction in the Thought World   ISBN: *1-59462-127-6* **$12.95** ☐
by *William Walker Atkinson*   Psychology/Religion Pages 144

Optimism by *Helen Keller*   ISBN: *1-59462-108-X* **$15.95** ☐
Helen Keller was blind, deaf, and mute since 19 months old, yet famously learned how to overcome these handicaps, communicate with the world, and spread her lectures promoting optimism. An inspiring read for everyone... Biographies/Inspirational Pages 84

Sara Crewe by *Frances Burnett*   ISBN: *1-59462-360-0* **$9.45** ☐
In the first place, Miss Minchin lived in London. Her home was a large, dull, tall one, in a large, dull square, where all the houses were alike, and all the sparrows were alike, and where all the door-knockers made the same heavy sound... Childrens/Classic Pages 88

The Autobiography of Benjamin Franklin by *Benjamin Franklin*   ISBN: *1-59462-135-7* **$24.95** ☐
The Autobiography of Benjamin Franklin has probably been more extensively read than any other American historical work, and no other book of its kind has had such ups and downs of fortune. Franklin lived for many years in England, where he was agent... Biographies/History Pages 332

Name	
Email	
Telephone	
Address	
City, State ZIP	

☐ **Credit Card**   ☐ **Check / Money Order**

Credit Card Number	
Expiration Date	
Signature	

Please Mail to: Book Jungle
PO Box 2226
Champaign, IL 61825
or Fax to: 630-214-0564

ORDERING INFORMATION

web: *www.bookjungle.com*
email: *sales@bookjungle.com*
fax: *630-214-0564*
mail: *Book Jungle PO Box 2226 Champaign, IL 61825*
or PayPal *to sales@bookjungle.com*

Please contact us for bulk discounts

DIRECT-ORDER TERMS

**20% Discount if You Order
Two or More Books**
Free Domestic Shipping!
Accepted: Master Card, Visa,
Discover, American Express

www.ingramcontent.com/pod-product-compliance
Lightning Source LLC
LaVergne TN
LVHW061226060426
835509LV00012B/1441